# BIOCHEMISTRY
## for advanced biology

**Susan Aldridge**

**CAMBRIDGE**
UNIVERSITY PRESS

Published by the Press Syndicate of the University of Cambridge
The Pitt Building, Trumpington Street, Cambridge CB2 1RP
40 West 20th Street, New York, NY 10011-4211, USA
10 Stamford Road, Oakleigh, Melbourne 3166, Australia

First published 1994

Printed in Great Britain at the University Press, Cambridge

A catalogue record for this book is available from the British Library

ISBN 0 521 437814 paperback

Cover photo: Geoff Tompkinson/Science Photo Library. This
composite image shows how a biochemist could use a virtual reality
system to investigate molecular interactions. The purple molecule is
HIV protease, the blue object is half a section of DNA.

Interior book design by Design/Section

Notice to teachers

# Contents

# Preface

Biology today is dominated by molecular biology – both in research and in its practical applications in medicine, agriculture and industry. An understanding of the biochemical principles that underpin molecular biology should be a part of any advanced biology course, not only to satisfy the requirements of the examination, but also to appreciate the impact of modern biology on society.

The aim of this book is to introduce students to these biochemical principles, emphasising practical applications and keeping chemical equations to a necessary minimum. Students without a background in chemistry should refer to the Appendix, which gives a brief summary of the chemistry required for this book.

The text fulfils the requirements of all the A level biology syllabuses for biochemistry and much of the biotechnology component. It is also suitable for students following BTEC courses in biological sciences and health sciences.

There is optional extension material, for students who wish to 'dig deeper'. Questions in the text are meant for homework/class discussion and answers are provided. There is a selection of recent A level examination questions at the end of each chapter.

# Acknowledgements

Thanks are due to Peter Byfield, David Martin, Katerina Michaelides and Paul Purkiss at the Clinical Research Centre for useful discussions, and to Stewart Humphrey of the Biochemical Society for background information.

The author and publishers are grateful to the following for permission to reproduce their photographs. Biophoto Associates 1.7c and 6.2a; J.C. Kendrew 2.14.

The examination questions at the end of each chapter are reproduced by the kind permission of International Baccalaureate Organisation (IB), Northern Examinations Assessment Board (NEAB), Oxford and Cambridge Schools Examinations Board (O&C), University of Cambridge Local Examinations Syndicate (UCLES), University of London Examinations and Assessment Council (London) and Welsh Joint Education Committee (WJEC).

# chapter 1

# Chemical reactions sustain the living cell

Biochemistry is the study of life itself, from a molecular point of view. Understanding how the molecules of life, such as proteins, work in the cell has been the major achievement of biology in the twentieth century. Although there is a great deal still to be discovered, biochemistry has already led to exciting discoveries in the world of medicine, industry and agriculture.

## 1.1 Life is based on carbon

Ninety-two of the chemical elements occur naturally on Earth, but only 16 of them are found in living organisms. Figure 1.1 shows that the distributions of the elements on Earth and in the human body are quite different. Silicon and metals make up nearly half of the Earth's crust but account for less than 5 per cent of our body mass. In fact, many metals, such as aluminium and mercury, are harmful to humans and other organisms. After oxygen, carbon is the most abundant element in living organisms. It is the unique chemical properties of carbon that make life possible.

The elements can be grouped together into families (or groups) whose members have similar chemical properties. Carbon and silicon are in the same family. Atoms of carbon and silicon are able to make four chemical bonds to other atoms. Carbon atoms form especially strong bonds with other carbon atoms (bond energy $346 \, \text{kJ mol}^{-1}$) as well as with hydrogen, oxygen and nitrogen atoms. This means that a huge number of different compounds containing rings and chains of carbon atoms are possible. To date, over 2.5 million carbon-based compounds have been recorded – greater than the number of compounds of all the other elements put together.

Even the simplest organisms contain thousands of carbon compounds. This might suggest that biochemistry is too complicated to be of any use. There are two reasons why this is not true. First, most of the complex compounds in the cell fall into one of only four chemical groups – **proteins**, **carbohydrates**, **lipids** and **nucleic acids**. Secondly, after over 50 years of studying the chemistry of the bacterium *Escherichia coli*, biochemists have come to the conclusion that living things have far more in common at the level of the cell than you might imagine from comparing their outer appearances. For example, both humans and many bacteria can use the same set of chemical reactions to extract energy from food.

Figure 1.1 The
distribution of
elements on
Earth and in
the human
body (by mass).

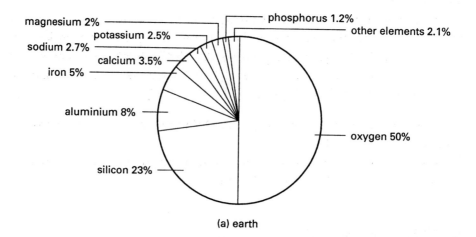

(a) earth

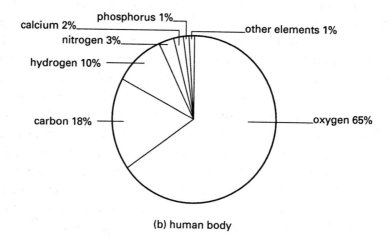

(b) human body

## Metabolism

More chemical activity goes on inside a living cell than in the most
sophisticated laboratory in the world. Complex molecules are built up from
simpler building blocks. For instance, the polymeric molecules of proteins,
carbohydrates and nucleic acids are assembled from their basic chemical units.
At the same time, other large molecules, such as foodstuffs, are broken down
into smaller ones. The sum total of the chemical activity that occurs in the cell
is known as **metabolism**.

Metabolic reactions are far more complicated than most of the chemical
reactions you might carry out in the laboratory, yet they occur readily at
relatively low temperatures. For example, the industrial preparation of
ammonia for the manufacture of fertilisers involves passing nitrogen and
hydrogen gases over an iron catalyst at a temperature of 450 °C and a pressure
of 200 atmospheres. Bacteria in the root nodules of leguminous plants can,

however, make ammonia from the nitrogen in the air at normal temperatures and pressures. It is the presence of the **enzyme**, nitrogenase, that makes this reaction possible. Enzymes are proteins that act as **catalysts** – they enable reactions to take place under relatively mild conditions. All biochemical reactions are catalysed by enzymes.

1 **Why is mercury harmful to living things? What other elements are toxic and what are their effects?**

2 **Discuss the feasibility of a life-form based on silicon instead of carbon. (Hint: the Si–Si bond energy is 226 kJ mol$^{-1}$.)**

QUESTIONS

## 1.2    How did it all start?

There has been life on Earth for at least 3.5 billion years. The evidence for this has come from the discovery of ancient **stromatolites** in Western Australia. Stromatolites are structures found in sedimentary rocks that are formed when cyanobacteria precipitate calcium carbonate (limestone) from sea water.

The Earth itself was formed between 4.5 and 5 billion years ago, and its atmosphere came from the gases that escaped from its hot liquid interior as the outer crust solidified. This mixture of gases was quite unlike the atmosphere today. No one knows the exact composition of the original atmosphere. It used to be thought that it consisted of methane, hydrogen, ammonia and water vapour. Some of the water vapour would have condensed to form the oceans. However, space travel has shown that our neighbouring planets have carbon dioxide atmospheres and many scientists now think that the carbon in the early Earth's atmosphere was present as carbon dioxide, not methane.

Free oxygen was absent, and so there was no ozone layer to absorb ultraviolet light from the Sun. (There would have been more lightning than there is today.) The Earth's surface would also have experienced heavy bombardment by meteorites during the final stages of formation of the Solar System.

How could living things be formed under such conditions? Again, it is impossible to be sure of the details, but the study of biochemistry has provided some important clues to the origin of life. Alexander Oparin, a Russian chemist, and the British scientist J. B. S. Haldane suggested that simple building blocks of the molecules found in living organisms were synthesised from chemicals in the early atmosphere. These substances then dissolved in the water of the oceans, forming a mixture whose chemical composition allowed the emergence of the first living organism. This mixture is often called the '**primeval soup**'.

In 1953, experiments by American chemists Harold Urey and Stanley Miller strengthened the hypothesis that the early Earth was a suitable

Figure 1.2 Urey
and Miller's
experiment.

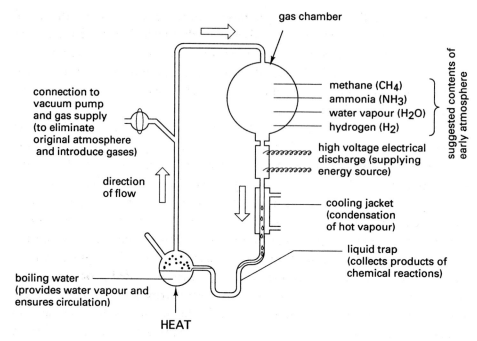

gas chamber

methane ($CH_4$)
ammonia ($NH_3$)
water vapour ($H_2O$)
hydrogen ($H_2$)

suggested contents of early atmosphere

connection to
vacuum pump
and gas supply
(to eliminate
original atmosphere
and introduce gases)

high voltage electrical
discharge (supplying
energy source)

direction
of flow

cooling jacket
(condensation
of hot vapour)

liquid trap
(collects products of
chemical reactions)

boiling water
(provides water vapour and
ensures circulation)

HEAT

laboratory for the synthesis of life's chemical building blocks. Figure 1.2 shows their simulation of the Earth of about 4 billion years ago. They made up a mixture of gases to represent the atmosphere. This mixture was circulated around the apparatus, passing through a reaction vessel where it was exposed to electric sparks, which were meant to simulate lightning. After running the experiment for a week, a variety of carbon compounds were found in the mixture. These included the amino acids, glycine and alanine, which are components of proteins.

Similar experiments have shown the formation of other important molecules – the bases that make up nucleic acids and the sugars that form carbohydrates, for example. The shock waves caused by the impact of meteorites and comets could have contributed some of the energy needed to form these carbon compounds. It is also possible that these impacts themselves could have showered the 'primeval soup' with amino acids and other carbon compounds. The appearance of Halley's comet in 1986 provided some evidence for this idea, as its dust was shown to contain large amounts of carbon compounds.

## Assembling life's ingredients

The presence of the right chemical mix in the 'primeval soup' is not enough, however, to explain how life began. First, simple chemicals cannot assemble themselves into complex molecules such as proteins without the help of enzymes. Secondly, as organic chemists know only too well, the usual outcome of mixing together chemicals such as those which might have been in the 'primeval soup' is a nasty black tar containing many different compounds – most of them unwanted. Finally, the violent conditions on the early Earth would have decomposed the amino acids and other molecules before any useful reactions could take place.

Many different theories have been put forward to try to solve these problems. An important step forward was the discovery, by American scientist Thomas Cech, that not all enzymes are proteins. One of the nucleic acids, **ribonucleic acid** (RNA), also has catalytic activity and could have helped to build the first cells. British scientist Graham Cairns-Smith has suggested that the first catalysts may not have been carbon-based at all; instead, clay particles in rocks could have helped to assemble the chemical components of cells.

Another idea is that life began in the cosy niches of hot springs on the ocean floor known as **hydrothermal vents**, which provided protection from the continual assault by giant meteorites. Research trips to hydrothermal vents show that these niches are teeming with life. The organisms that live there do not need sunlight for energy – instead they use chemicals that are emitted from cracks in the ocean floor. This ability would have been a valuable asset on the early Earth, as meteoritic impacts could have thrown up enough dust into the atmosphere to stop sunlight reaching the surface.

Some scientists – notably British astronomer Fred Hoyle, and Nobel Prizewinner Francis Crick – suggest that life did not originate on Earth at all. Hoyle says that microbes floating in space provided the 'seeds of life' on Earth – a theory known as **panspermia**. Crick has suggested that there was plenty of time (10 billion years) for life to originate on some other planet before it did on Earth, and that the 'seeds of life' were sent here in a spaceship.

Although most scientists dismiss Hoyle and Crick's ideas, NASA, the American space agency, is expanding its search for life on other planets. SETI (the search for extra-terrestrial intelligence) will survey radio signals from 700 stars, which may be orbited by planets similar to our own.

**3 Is Urey and Miller's experiment a good model of the early Earth? Can you suggest any ways of improving it or using it to test other ideas about the origin of life?**   QUESTION

## 1.3   Life needs the right environment

Life can only flourish if the conditions both outside and inside the organism are suitable. External conditions include temperature, atmospheric pressure and composition. Table 1.1 shows how conditions on Earth compare with those on our neighbouring planets, Mars and Venus.

**Table 1.1   Percentage gas composition and temperatures of planetary atmospheres**

| Gas | Venus | Mars | Earth |
|---|---|---|---|
| Carbon dioxide | 96.5% | 95% | 0.03% |
| Nitrogen | 3.5% | 2.7% | 79% |
| Oxygen | – | – | 21% |
| Temperature | 459°C | −53°C | 13°C |

As we have seen, life evolved in the absence of oxygen, so there is no unique atmospheric composition that is required to support life. Temperature is a more crucial factor. The freezing of water at 0°C sets a lower temperature limit on life processes. These processes are controlled by enzymes, and most enzymes are inactivated at temperatures above 50°C. This sets an upper limit to the temperature range that can support life.

However, some species have evolved ways of exceeding these limitations. Antarctic fish, for example, which survive at temperatures below 0°C, have 'anti-freeze' proteins in their blood that stop ice crystals forming. The bacterium *Thermophilus aquaticus* has heat-stable enzymes that enable it to live in hot springs at temperatures around 90°C.

## Elemental cycles

The elements that are essential to life are present in fixed amounts on the Earth. They are, however, recycled – continually changing their chemical state as they are transferred from the environment to living things and back again. This recycling relies upon biochemical processes, especially those which take place in bacteria and fungi. The most important **elemental cycles** are those involving carbon, nitrogen, sulphur and phosphorus (Figure 1.3–1.6). (The numbers on the drawings correspond to those used here in the text.)

### Carbon   (Figure 1.3)

1   Carbon dioxide ($CO_2$) in the atmosphere, or dissolved in water, is the most important carbon source for living organisms.

2   Carbon dioxide is 'fixed' by green plants during **photosynthesis**, forming carbohydrates, fats and proteins. These carbon compounds enter other organisms when plants are consumed.

3   **Respiration**, the process by which cells extract energy from food, returns carbon dioxide to the atmosphere. Bacteria and fungi known as **decomposers** turn complex molecules from dead organisms into simpler ones, releasing carbon dioxide into the atmosphere in the process.

4   Some carbon remains trapped in dead organisms in low-oxygen environments such as water-logged soil. Over a period of millions of years, fossil fuels are formed from these organic remains.

5   Burning these fuels also adds carbon dioxide to the atmosphere.

6   Carbon dioxide dissolved in water eventually forms sedimentary rocks.

7   These rocks eventually return their carbon dioxide to the atmosphere by weathering – a gradual decomposition of the rock brought about by exposure to wind, rain, sun and microbial action. Volcanic eruptions can add very large amounts of carbon dioxide to the atmosphere.

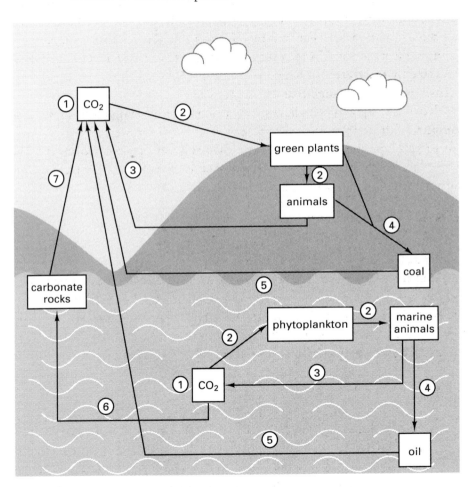

**Figure 1.3**

**Carbon cycle**

**The greenhouse effect**   Carbon dioxide is one of several 'green-house' gases in the Earth's atmosphere. Greenhouse gases trap heat energy that would otherwise be reflected from the Earth out into space. Without this greenhouse effect, the Earth's temperature would be too low to support life (note the powerful greenhouse effect on Venus). But the amount of carbon dioxide and other greenhouse gases in the Earth's atmosphere has increased over the last 100 years, mainly because of human activities such as agriculture and the burning of fossil fuels. The temperature of the Earth has also increased by about 0.5 °C, and most scientists now predict a further sharp rise between 1.5 and 4.5 °C within the next century. The effects of this **global warming** are difficult to assess, but are likely to include widespread climatic change. How living organisms will respond to this change in their environment is even harder to predict.

## Nitrogen

**Figure 1.4**

**Nitrogen cycle**

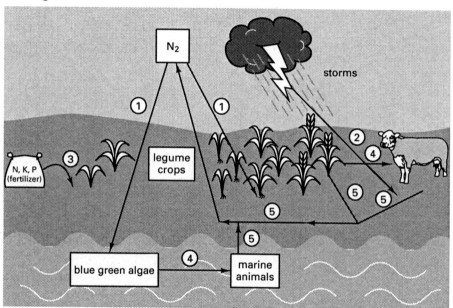

1   Nitrogen makes up 79 per cent of our atmosphere, but occurs as the free element, which is an unreactive gas ($N_2$) that cannot be used directly by living things. It can, however, be converted into nitrogen-containing compounds such as nitrates and ammonia, which can be absorbed by plants. This process is known as **nitrogen fixation**. Most nitrogen fixation occurs through the action of bacteria and blue-green algae. These organisms contain an enzyme called **nitrogenase** that is able to convert nitrogen into ammonia. Bacteria of the *Rhizobium* genus live in nodules on the roots of leguminous plants in a **symbiotic relationship** where the plant provides the bacteria with food and the bacteria transfer ammonia to the plant. Nitrogen fixation by free-living blue-green algae is an important source of nitrogen for aquatic organisms.

2    A small amount of nitrogen fixation also occurs when the energy
of lightning flashes is used to form nitrogen oxides from nitrogen
and oxygen in the atmosphere. These oxides dissolve in rain
water, forming nitric acid, which turns to nitrates in the soil.

3    Nitrates may also be added directly to the soil by the application
of fertilisers.

4    Plants convert nitrates and ammonia into more complex
molecules – in particular, proteins and nucleic acids – and supply
these, in turn, to animals.

5    When organisms decay, nitrogen-containing compounds are
processed by soil microbes. Decomposers turn them into
ammonia, which is converted back into nitrates by **nitrifying
bacteria**. Then they are transformed into nitrogen by **denitrifying
bacteria**, which complete the cycle.

## Sulphur

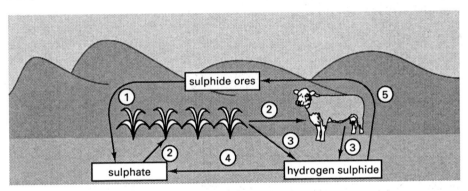

**Figure 1.5**

**Sulphur cycle**

1    The main source of sulphur is not the atmosphere, but rocks
containing ores such as pyrites (iron sulphide). Bacteria turn
sulphide into sulphate.

2    Sulphate is readily taken up by living organisms. The sulphur
atoms in sulphate are then incorporated into proteins.

3    Decomposing bacteria extract sulphur from dead and waste
matter, converting it into hydrogen sulphide ($H_2S$) – with its
characteristic smell of rotten eggs.

4    This can be turned back into sulphate by bacterial action for
re-use.

5    Other bacteria, living in hot springs, turn hydrogen sulphide into
sulphur, which is then stored in sediments, completing the cycle.

## Phosphorus

Figure 1.6

Phosphorus

cycle

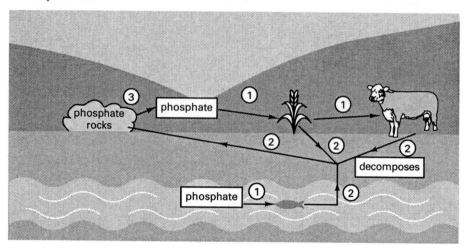

1   Phosphates in soil and water are incorporated into living
    organisms where phosphorus is a vital component of nucleic acids
    and other compounds.
2   Decomposers return phosphorus to the environment as
    phosphate, which may be deposited in rocks.
3   Weathering leads to the release of phosphates to soil and water.

Both environmental and microbial processes play an important part in cycling
these elements, all of which – as shown in Figure 1.1 – are essential to life.

QUESTION    **4 An amateur winemaker tries to make wine from the following recipe:**
            **1 kg sucrose**
            **5 g dried yeast**
            **4 dm³ sterilised water**
            **No wine is formed. What remedy would you suggest? (Hint: the yeast has**
            **requirements that are similar to those of any other living organism.)**

### 1.4   The inner environment

The environment inside a living organism has to be carefully controlled for
biochemical reactions to take place. These conditions are geared to the
requirements of enzymes. Most enzymes are sensitive to heat, and to extremes
of acidity or alkalinity (this will be discussed further in Chapter 2 and 9).

Fluids in which biochemical reactions take place are usually **buffered**. This
means that their chemical composition is such that they can resist small
additions of acid or alkali; they tend to maintain a constant pH. For example,

blood plasma is slightly alkaline, with a pH of 7.4. Respiration produces carbon dioxide, which gives a weakly acidic solution of carbonic acid in plasma according to the reaction:

$$CO_2 + H_2O \quad \rightarrow \quad H_2CO_3 \quad \rightleftharpoons \quad H^+ + HCO_3^-$$

| in blood | carbonic acid | hydrogen carbonate ion |

The hydrogen ions produced in this reaction would make the blood acidic were it not for the buffering action of sodium hydrogencarbonate in the plasma, which mops up the hydrogen ions in the following reaction:

$$HCO_3^- + H^+ \rightleftharpoons H_2CO_3$$

The addition of alkali, as hydroxide ions, would lead to the following reaction:

$$HCO_3^- + OH^- \rightleftharpoons H_2O + CO_3^{2-}$$

carbonate ion

So the addition of acids and alkalis to blood plasma does not cause any significant change in pH. Other substances with a buffering action include amino acids, proteins and phosphate ions.

Maintaining the pH of blood is an important concern for patients during operations where breathing is taken over by a mechanical ventilator. In these cases, medical laboratory scientists are on hand to monitor the amount of carbon dioxide present in the blood. The gases supplied by the 'heart–lung' machine can be adjusted to take care of any pH problem that might arise.

The temperature and fluid composition of living organisms are kept constant by a variety of mechanisms, depending upon the organism's complexity. For multicellular organisms, this maintenance of a constant inner environment is known as **homeostasis**.

## Water, and other essential ingredients

Water is essential to life as it provides a medium in which biochemical reactions can take place. Because of its solvent properties, water can dissolve a wide range of substances of biological importance, from sodium chloride to proteins. When large molecules such as proteins dissolve in water, a fluid called a **colloid** is formed in which the protein is surrounded by a 'shell' of water molecules.

Living organisms need more than just the complex carbon-based molecules to function. Some small carbon compounds are also required, many of which are derived from vitamins. Also, a variety of inorganic ions are necessary, including calcium, magnesium, sodium and chloride, and trace elements such as manganese and copper.

QUESTION   **5 Water accounts for about 75 per cent of the mass of most cells. How would you confirm this? Why do leafy vegetables such as spinach 'collapse' when they are cooked, and why do frozen strawberries not taste like fresh ones?**

## 1.5   The world of the cell

The **cell** is a compartment that contains the chemicals taking part in the reactions that sustain life and it separates these chemicals from the outer environment. Without the barrier of the cell membrane, the chemicals would drift apart and no reactions would take place.

Molecules from the 'primeval soup' had to group together, separating themselves from their surroundings, before life could start to evolve. Alexander Oparin, building on his earlier ideas about the origin of life, suggested that proteins (once they were synthesised from amino acids) might have formed droplets known as **coacervates**. Using the protein, gelatin, and gum arabic, a carbohydrate, he formed droplets that behaved like primitive cells. If an enzyme was trapped inside a droplet, for example, it acted upon chemicals that diffused in from the surroundings.

Robert Hooke, the English scientist and inventor, first described cells in the 1660s as a result of his studies with the recently discovered microscope. But it was not until the nineteenth century that scientists realised the true significance of cells. In 1838, a German botanist, Matthias Schleiden, suggested that all plant tissues are made of cells. The following year his friend, Theodor Schwann, went further by saying that all life-forms were built of cells. 'The organism', he said, 'is a cellular state in which each cell is a citizen.' But biologists were still not sure where cells actually came from. A popular idea was 'spontaneous generation' in which life could be created suddenly – apparently from nothing. Then experiments by Louis Pasteur and Rudolf Virchow showed that cells could only come from other living cells. When Pasteur carefully sterilised a flask of nutrient broth – so that it was free of microbes – no new organisms appeared. But if the flask was exposed to the air, colonies of microbes grew very quickly, because the flask had been contaminated by air-borne organisms. These observations completed the cell theory, with its central idea that the cell is the basic unit of an organism.

**Table 1.2    Sizes of atoms, molecules and cells (in nanometres)**

|  | Approximate diameter/nm |
| --- | --- |
| Hydrogen atom | 0.1 |
| Protein molecule | 10 |
| Bacterial cell | 1000 |
| Animal cell | 10 000–30 000 |
| Plant cell | 10 000–100 000 |

The cell is the basis of living things in the same way as atoms are the basis of matter. But atoms are many orders of magnitude smaller than cells. Table 1.2 gives the relative sizes of atoms, molecules and cells.

The cell is like a small-scale chemical laboratory where thousands of different reactions are being carried out. These include the synthesis of proteins and the dismantling of foodstuffs to extract energy and nutrients. There are two basic types of cell – **prokaryotic** and **eukaryotic**. Organisms made up of these types of cells are known as prokaryotes and eukaryotes respectively. Prokaryotes, such as bacteria, are usually single-celled organisms. Eukaryotes can be as simple as yeast, or as complex as plants or humans. The prokaryotic cell came first in evolution and does not have a nucleus (Figure 1.7c). Eukaryotic cells are larger and more complex (Figures 1.7a and b).

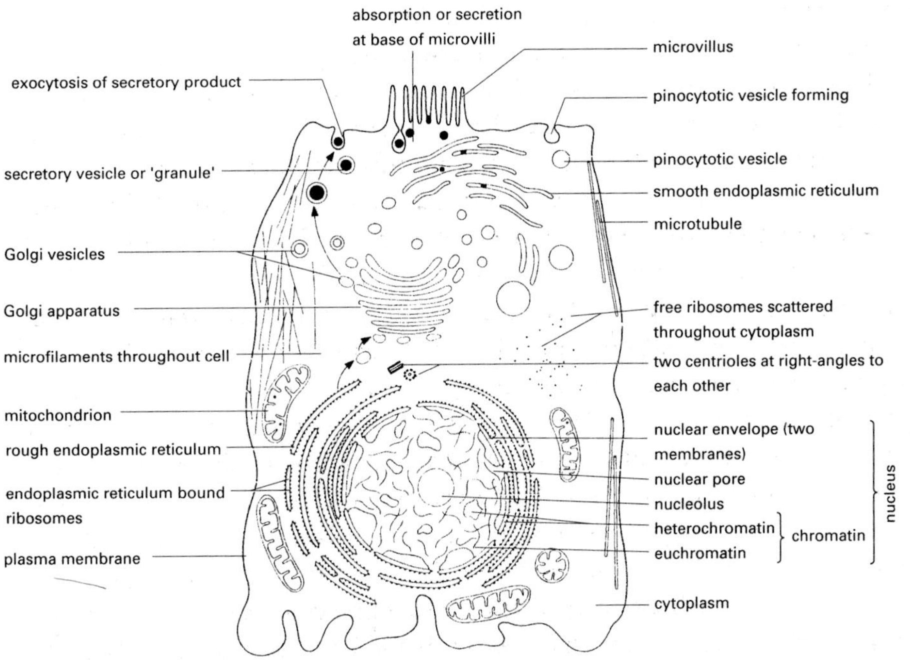

**Figure 1.7 (a) A typical animal cell.**

**(b) A typical plant cell.**

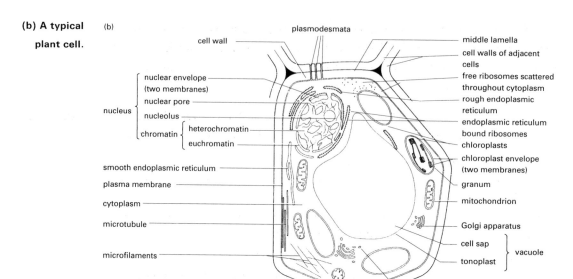

(b)

plasmodesmata

cell wall

middle lamella

cell walls of adjacent cells

free ribosomes scattered throughout cytoplasm

rough endoplasmic reticulum

nucleus
- nuclear envelope (two membranes)
- nuclear pore
- nucleolus
- chromatin
  - heterochromatin
  - euchromatin

endoplasmic reticulum bound ribosomes

chloroplasts

chloroplast envelope (two membranes)

smooth endoplasmic reticulum

granum

plasma membrane

mitochondrion

cytoplasm

Golgi apparatus

microtubule

cell sap

vacuole

microfilaments

tonoplast

Golgi vestcle

**(c) Electron micrograph of a section of a typical rod-shaped bacterium, *Bacillus subtilis* (magnification about 25 000).**

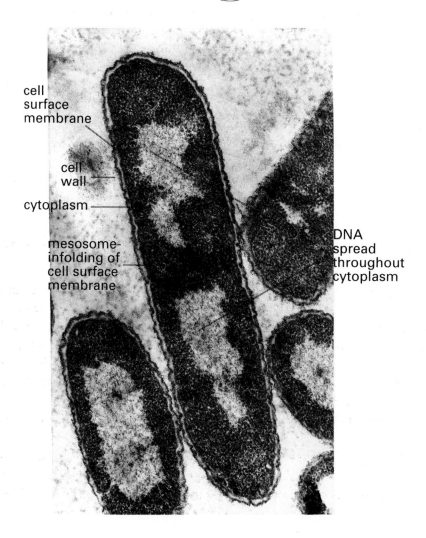

cell surface membrane

cell wall

cytoplasm

mesosome-infolding of cell surface membrane

DNA spread throughout cytoplasm

Besides a nucleus, they also possess a number of smaller structures known as **organelles**, each dedicated to an individual task. These are shown in Figure 1.7 and described in Table 1.3. The last three organelles listed in the table are found only in plants.

**6** Find out the functions of organelles not listed in Table 1.3 and list the main structural differences between prokaryotic and eukaryotic cells.

QUESTION

**Table 1.3   Organelles and their functions**

| Organelle | Function |
| --- | --- |
| Nucleus | control of cellular activity |
| Nucleolus | manufactures ribosomes |
| Ribosomes | the site of protein manufacture (found in both prokaryotes and eukaryotes) |
| Endoplasmic reticulum | protein transport and lipid synthesis |
| Golgi apparatus | processing of cell materials, such as enzymes |
| Lysosomes | breakdown of cell materials |
| Mitochondria | site of latter stages of respiration |
| Microtubules | support cell, forming 'cytoskeleton' |
| Vacuole | storage of products, including waste |
| Tonoplast | vacuole membrane |
| Chloroplast | photosynthesis |

## 1.6   Cells and their products are the basis of the biotechnology industry

The growth of large populations of microbes such as yeast in nutrient solutions has a long history, but it is only in the twentieth century that techniques for growing cells from more complex organisms have been developed. **Cell culture** (sometimes also known as **tissue culture**) involves growing animal or plant cells in a nutrient medium. Tissue from the organism is first treated with enzymes to separate the cells. These are then allowed to grow and divide in a sterile culture medium, which contains a carefully balanced mixture of nutrients. The pH and temperature are monitored as the cells grow.

Animal and plant cells grow more slowly than microbes, often taking several hours to divide. Animal cells often stop growing after a few cell divisions, unless they come from tumour tissue. These cells are said to be

**transformed** and will grow and divide indefinitely. Plant cells can be grown into complete organisms – a process known as **regeneration** – if hormones are added to the culture at the right stage. These plants are known as **clones** of the original, because they have the same genetic make-up. This type of cloning does not occur naturally in animals, because the genes of animals are controlled differently as the organism develops. The cloning of animals – such as frogs – has been achieved, but it is technically very difficult. However, advanced techniques for handling and manipulating animal cells may make the cloning of animals a practical possibility in the future.

Besides offering the possibility of cloned plants, cells have a variety of other uses. Animal cells are used in medical research for the study of viruses and the production of vaccines. Microbes are used to clean up pollution and to tackle other environmental problems. Many cell types can be used in new methods of toxicity testing, and some manufacture useful products such as antibiotics, flavours and dyes.

## Cloned oil palms

Many plants including orchids, potatoes and chrysanthemums can be cloned from tissue culture. The aim is usually to obtain very large numbers of high-yielding, disease-free plants. One of the most ambitious cloning projecs to date comes from the international company Unilever. The company has an interest in oil palm plantations in Africa, Malaysia and Colombia.

The oil palm produces two sorts of oil – palm oil and palm kernel oil – which have a wide range of uses in the food and chemical industries. For example, palm oil is used as a cooking oil, and in margarine, ice cream and baking fat. It has been promoted for its health benefits because it contains substances, such as beta-carotene, that may protect against cancer. Like many other plant oils, palm oils can also be used in the chemical industry, as an

**Figure 1.8 Cloning oil palm – from cells to plantlets.**

1. Roots are taken from a high-yielding oil palm

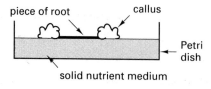

piece of root    callus

Petri dish

solid nutrient medium

2. Pieces of root are placed on solid nutrient medium. The root cells multiply and form a mass of tissue called CALLUS

3. Pieces of callus removed and 'grown on'

4. Addition of hormones leads to development of roots and shoots

plantlets

5. Plantlets are 'grown on' in individual test tubes of nutrient, before planting out

alternative to petroleum in the production of plastics, for example. Palm kernel oil is used in the manufacture of soap – and there is renewed interest in developing new types of soaps as an alternative to petroleum-based detergents.

Unilever aims to boost production of palm oils from 3.5 to 5 tonnes per hectare by making clones of high-yielding palms using the technique shown in Figure 1.8. The project is a long-term one with large-scale plantations of the clones set to produce oil by the end of the century. At present, Unilever palm oil accounts for only 1–2 per cent of the world palm oil market. Cloning could change this, and the resulting impact on the world oil trade may be considerable.

## Metabolic factories

The metabolic reactions of the cell result in a wide range of chemical products known as **metabolites**. Some of these, such as amino acids, are essential for the cell's survival. These are called **primary metabolites**. But microbes and plants, in particular, make other substances known as **secondary metabolites**, which are of no immediate use to them. Ever since the ancient Egyptians used

**Table 1.4   Some secondary metabolites from microbes and plants**

| Metabolite(s) | Organism of origin | Property/use |
|---|---|---|
| *Microbial metabolites* | | |
| Penicillin | *Penicillium chrysogenum* | antibiotic |
| Fusaric acid | *Fusarium* species | lowers blood pressure |
| 1,3-Diphenethylurea | *Streptomyces* species | anti-depressant |
| Geraniol | *Ceratocystis variospora* | rose aroma |
| Ethyl butyrate | *Lactobacillus casei* | fruity flavour |
| Gibberellins | *Gibberella fujikuroi* | plant hormones |
| Piericidin | *Streptomyces mobaraensis* | insecticide |
| *Plant metabolites* | | |
| Codeine | poppy | analgesic |
| Diosgenin | yam | contraceptive |
| Quinine | cinchona | anti-malarial |
| Digoxin | foxglove | treatment of heart failure |
| Vincristine | rosy periwinkle | leukaemia treatment |
| Pyrethrin | chrysanthemum | insecticide |
| Shikonin | *Lithospermum erythrorhizon* (a wild herb native to Japan) | red dye |

mouldy bread – with its coating of penicillin – to treat infected wounds, humans have made use of secondary metabolites, some of which are listed in Table 1.4.

Microbial metabolites are manufactured by culturing specially selected high-yielding strains of the microbes in a giant vessel known as a fermenter. At present, it is more difficult to produce plant metabolites from cells in culture than from the whole plant. Shikonin – which is used to colour both lipstick and the Japanese national flag – and vanilla are the only plant products that have been produced in commercial quantities by cell culture.

**QUESTION**   **7 Give one reason why it might be hard to produce metabolites from plant cells in culture.**

## Penicillin production

The antibiotic **penicillin** was discovered in 1928 by the Scottish bacteriologist, Alexander Fleming. For several years he had been searching for a substance that could kill bacteria. A culture dish of *Staphylococcus* bacteria in his laboratory became contaminated with an air-borne mould, *Penicillium notatum*. Fleming noticed that the growth of the bacteria was slowed by a substance produced by the mould. He named this substance penicillin. Ten years later Howard Florey and Ernest Chain purified and characterised penicillin and tested it on patients. The three scientists were rewarded by a Nobel Prize in 1945 for one of the most important discoveries in twentieth-century medicine.

Penicillin works by stopping the synthesis of cell walls in a wide range of bacteria. Without a cell wall, the bacteria burst in a normal fluid medium. Although penicillin is not generally toxic to humans, some people are allergic to it. Bacteria can also become resistant to penicillin, particularly in situations where it is over-prescribed.

There is now a wide variety of penicillin-like and other antibiotics available, but penicillin G was the first to be produced commercially. The development of large-scale penicillin production in the 1940s was driven by the need for antibiotics in the Second World War. Fleming's original mould was replaced by *Penicillium chrysogenum*, which was isolated from a mouldy melon on a market stall in Peoria, Illinois, USA, when the original production team enrolled the general public in the search for a higher-yielding strain.

Spores of *P. chrysogenum* are incubated to make a starter culture, which is then added to a sterile medium in a fermentation vessel, which could have a volume of up to 200 000 litres. The medium includes glucose or molasses as a carbon source, while nitrogen is provided by corn-steep liquor, a waste product from the extraction of starch from maize. The mixture is agitated and aerated, the pH and temperature being controlled throughout by a computer. Sterility must be carefully maintained by steam sterilisation of the empty vessel and culture medium as well as filtration of the air before it enters the vessel. Research has shown that the fermentation proceeds in two phases – a period of rapid growth, followed by one of much slower growth. It is in this latter period that most of the penicillin is produced.

When the fermentation is over, the products are filtered to remove the filamentous *P. chrysogenum* and the filtrate is chilled and acidified. Chilling is necessary because penicillin decomposes at room temperature in solutions of low pH. The penicillin is removed from the filtrate by extraction into an organic solvent. This is extracted back into aqueous buffer and, if the solution is concentrated enough, the penicillin will precipitate out at this stage. If it does not precipitate, the solvent extraction steps are repeated until it does. The organic solvents are then recycled by distillation.

**8  Draw a flowchart to show all the operations involved in penicillin production. List the ways in which the yield can be maximised and the operating costs minimised.**    QUESTION

## Environmental biotechnology

Microbes can use a wide variety of carbon and energy sources. This has led to their employment in a number of techniques for dealing with environmental pollution. Microbes can treat waste water, contaminated land and oil spills by degrading or mineralising toxic carbon compounds to carbon dioxide and water. For example, the sites of former gas works that are contaminated with oil and tar can be restored in a matter of months by microbial action. Polluted waste streams from pesticide factories can be cleaned up in minutes when they are passed through columns with microbes immobilised on an inert support. These new technologies are cheap and effective, and could be transferred easily to developing countries.

Toxic heavy metals such as mercury and uranium can also be dealt with by microbes in a process known as **biosorption**. Certain substances, such as the carbohydrate **chitin**, in the cell walls of the microbes bind strongly to the metal ions, and can pull them out of the waste streams of the nuclear, electroplating and metal-processing industries. The British Textile Technology Group is working on filters made of fungi for this purpose. When liquid industrial waste is passed through these filters, most of the contaminating metal ions are removed.

Some bacteria, such as *Thiobacillus ferroxidans*, can use metal ions as a source of energy. *Thiobacillus* uses iron sulphide in rocks in this way, releasing sulphuric acid as a by-product. This process is responsible for the blue streams of copper sulphate seen where low-grade copper ores occur, such as the Rio Tinto mine in south-west Spain. Copper ions are mobilised by the sulphuric acid and leached out of the rocks. Pure copper can easily be extracted from the copper sulphate solution.

Not only does this microbial mining avoid the sulphur dioxide pollution associated with conventional copper extraction, it also lowers the production costs.

QUESTION

**9 A school is to be built on the site of a former chemical factory. The soil on the site is found to be contaminated with a carbon-based compound known as pentachlorophenol (PCP), which is an ingredient of the wood preservative that the factory used to manufacture. You are the research director of an environmental biotechnology company and have been asked to solve the problem. Outline your strategy.**

## Alternatives to animals

Since the development of the petrochemicals industry in the 1940s, an increasing volume of synthetic chemicals has been introduced into our everyday lives. Each new chemical has to be tested for any harmful effects. Usually these tests are carried out on animals. But the numbers of animals used in testing have fallen in recent years – new in vitro testing methods based on cell cultures are partly responsible for this.

For example, some drugs have to be tested for endotoxins (substances produced by bacteria), because these can cause fever – as they do in cholera and typhoid. Until the development of the cell-based LAL test, rabbits were injected with the test drug and examined for signs of fever. (LAL stands for *Limulus* amoebocyte lysate – the blood cells of the horseshoe crab or *Limulus* are known as amoebocytes.) When an extract (or lysate) of these cells is mixed in a test tube with the test drug, a clot forms if endotoxin is present, as shown in Figure 1.9. Meanwhile, the crab is returned, unharmed, to the sea.

## The Ames test

The Ames test uses a specially selected strain of *Salmonella* bacteria to test for **mutagens** – chemicals that increase the frequency of mutations in DNA. It has been found that many (but not all) mutagens cause cancer in humans and other animals. The Ames test – named after the American biochemist Bruce Ames, who first published details of it in 1975 – is very widely used as a screen for chemicals as they are being developed for a variety of uses. It cuts down on the number of animal tests and gives an early indication of chemicals that may be harmful and are not worth developing any further.

The *Salmonella* bacteria used in the Ames test have two special characteristics. First, they cannot make the amino acid, histidine. It must be supplied in their growth medium, or they will die. Secondly, their cell membranes are rather leaky, making it easy for chemicals to pass inside.

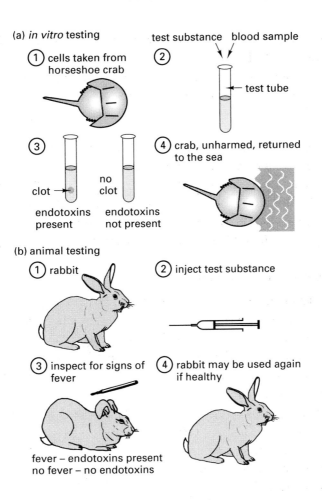

Figure 1.9 *In vitro* versus animal testing.

The *Salmonella* are grown in Petri dishes containing **minimal medium** (which includes only substances essential for growth) and just a little histidine. Test chemicals are applied to the dishes. Mutagens will mutate the histidine-requiring bacteria to a form that can make its own histidine. This process is called **reversion** and the bacteria produced are **revertants**. They form colonies, which can be counted on the dish. The more mutagenic the chemical is, the more colonies there will be.

Some innocent chemicals only become mutagenic once they have been metabolised by enzymes in the liver. These substances do not escape detection in the Ames test, however. A mixture of liver enzymes is added to the test mixture to simulate the effect of the liver on these potential mutagens. This means that any chemicals that become mutagenic only after being processed by the liver will also test positive.

QUESTION   10 The following results were obtained from the Ames test for three different substances A, B and C. The strain used has a spontaneous reversion rate of 30 colonies under the conditions of the experiment.
A: 32 colonies
B: 100 colonies
C: no growth
Explain these results. Describe the control experiment(s) you would set up and any further experiments you could do to find out more about the three substances.

## 1.7   The cell needs a power supply

The busy world of the cell would run down and stop without a power supply. Some organisms obtain their energy directly from the Sun, while others use chemical energy stored in fuels such as glucose to power their activity.

This chemical energy is extracted by a process known as **respiration**. Respiration differs in a number of ways from the combustion that occurs when a fuel such as methane is burned. Respiration occurs in several stages, it involves many catalysts (enzymes), and the energy is not released in the burst of heat and light of a flame but is transferred instead to a chemical called **adenosine triphosphate (ATP)**, which is found in all cells.

### The importance of ATP

Biochemists often refer to ATP as the 'energy currency' of the cell. It provides energy when the following hydrolysis reaction, which is catalysed by an enzyme called ATPase, takes place:

$$\text{ATP} + \text{H}_2\text{O} \rightarrow \text{ADP} + \text{P} + \text{energy}$$

| adenosine triphosphate | | | adenosine diphosphate | phosphate | 31 kJ mol$^{-1}$ |

This reaction is coupled to reactions that require energy, so that the energy released by the ATP is promptly channelled into other chemical bonds. ATP hydrolysis also powers muscle contraction, the pumping of ions across membranes (necessary for the transmission of nerve impulses) and the control of the water content of cells. The details of how ATP is generated from respiration and photosynthesis are given in Chapter 6.

There are two kinds of respiration – **aerobic**, which requires oxygen and produces carbon dioxide and water, and **anaerobic**, which can occur in the absence of oxygen and does not break down the glucose molecule completely. Aerobic respiration can produce 38 molecules of ATP for one molecule of glucose. The initial stage of respiration – glycolysis – takes place in the cytoplasm. Aerobic respiration is then completed in the mitochondria, where most of the ATP is generated.

Anaerobic respiration is often known as **fermentation** and can produce a variety of simple substances, such as ethanol, lactic acid and ethanoic acid, from glucose and other carbohydrates. Some of these have a commercial value, and air will be carefully excluded from the fermentation vessel to maximise the yield (even though from the cell's point of view fermentation is inefficient because it does not maximise the production of ATP). One new product of fermentation is the polymer polyhydroxybutyrate (PHB). PHB is produced commercially from the bacterium *Alcaligenes eutrophus* under the name 'Biopol'. Biopol is a biodegradable plastic, which can replace polythene in shampoo bottles and other containers. It is not, as yet, widely available, but it has the potential to replace conventional plastics, which are not easily broken down by microbes when they are discarded.

## Energy from the Sun

The cells of green plants and some bacteria carry out photosynthesis, a process in which glucose is synthesised from carbon dioxide and water using the energy of sunlight. ATP is also produced. All life on Earth is dependent on photosynthesis because it leads ultimately to the production of nearly all the carbon compounds found in organisms. The overall reaction is:

$$6CO_2 + 6H_2O \rightarrow C_6H_{12}O_6 + 6O_2$$

glucose

The details of photosynthesis are given in Chapter 6.

Organisms that use photosynthesis as a source of energy and food are known as **autotrophs**. As well as green plants they include blue-green algae (cyanobacteria), halobacteria and the green and purple bacteria. Photosynthesis by cyanobacteria was responsible for the accumulation of oxygen in the atmosphere, which began about 3 billion years ago. The basic mechanism of photosynthesis is similar in all these organisms, but green and purple bacteria use a pigment called **bacteriochlorophyll**, whereas the halobacteria use a specialised pigment known as **bacteriorhodopsin**. In plants, photosynthesis takes place in chloroplasts, where **chlorophyll** is concentrated. Bacteria have no chloroplasts; instead, the photosynthetic pigments are embedded in the cell membrane.

**11** 'Life found deep beneath the Earth.' Read the newspaper cutting. List the energy, nutrient and other requirements of these organisms and outline how you would assess these in the laboratory.    QUESTION

# Life found deep beneath the Earth

SCIENTISTS have discovered live bacteria several miles below ground that have apparently lived off energy from the Earth's core for millions of years. Other researchers have previously reported microbes living at about 200 metres below the seabed, but this is the first time that live bacteria have been discovered at great depths in ancient granite rock.

The discovery of the deepest living organisms could upset existing theories on the origin of life, which invoke the importance of the Sun's energy in sustaining organisms. Unlike life-forms on the surface of the planet, the subterranean bacteria seem not to have relied on the Sun's energy for their survival. They could be a model for possible underground life on other planets, Thomas Gold, emeritus professor of astronomy at Cornell University, New York, said yesterday.

The amount of life existing deep underground could exceed that living on or near the Earth's surface, he said. 'We do not know at present how to make a realistic estimate of the subterranean mass of material now living, but all that can be said is that one must consider it possible that it is comparable to all the living mass at the surface.... There are certainly very major life-forms down there.'

There are at least ten other planets or their moons in the Solar System where similar subterranean microbes could exist, he said.

Ulrich Szewzyk, a microbiologist at Sweden's National Bacteriological Laboratory in Stockholm, has cultured several strains of new bacteria from samples of granite rock taken from a borehole at depths of between five and six kilometres, Professor Gold says in the current issue of the *Proceedings of the National Academy of Sciences*.

The borehole was drilled in an ancient crater in central Sweden called the Siljan Ring, caused by the impact of a massive meteorite millions of years ago. Because the rock is granite, and not sedimentary deposits such as sandstone, it is unlikely the microbes originated from life on the surface, Professor Gold said. The bacteria do not need oxygen and live at very high temperatures of about 100 °C.

Dr Szewzyk has written a 'very substantial' scientific paper on the discovery and, co-operating with Carl Woese, Professor of Microbiology at the University of Illinois, will submit it later this year to the US National Academy of Sciences for publication.

Steve Connor, *The Independent*, 2 July 1992, p. 1

## Summary of Chapter 1

1  The most important elements in living organisms are oxygen, carbon, hydrogen, nitrogen, calcium and phosphorus. The complexity of life on Earth is based upon the unique chemical properties of carbon, which forms strong chemical bonds with itself and with hydrogen. The main classes of molecules found in living things are proteins, carbohydrates and lipids, along with smaller molecules and ions. Living organisms share many common metabolic pathways.

2  Life probably arose from the synthesis of simple building blocks such as amino acids and sugars in the oceans about 3.8 billion years ago. There are many theories that suggest how these building blocks organised themselves into the first cells.

3  Carbon, nitrogen, sulphur and phosphorus are continually recycled between living things and their environment. Biochemical processes play an important role in this.

4  Biochemical reactions take place in an aqueous environment whose temperature, composition and pH are controlled by homeostasis.

5   The cell is the fundamental unit of living organisms. Biochemical functions are localised in units within the cells called organelles. Prokaryotes are cells without nuclei. Eukaryotes have nuclei and a more complex internal structure than prokaryotes.

6   Cells can be grown in culture. There are many applications of cultured cells including cloned plants, the production of antibiotics and other chemicals, degradation of chemical pollution and toxicity testing.

7   Most organisms obtain their energy directly or indirectly from the Sun, via photosynthesis. ATP is the chemical energy source that drives chemical reactions in the cell. It is synthesised in cells either by respiration or by photosynthesis.

## Examination questions

1   Describe the processes by which nitrogen and carbon circulate in the biosphere. (WJEC, part of question)

2   Give an account of:
(a) the use of bacteria for metal leaching and recovery,
(b) plant tissue culture,
referring to production methods and commercial applications involved. (JMB, now NEAB, A/S)

3   'Changes in the atmosphere due to human activities will have major biological effects unless reversed.' Discuss this statement with reference to named examples. (London)

4   Describe the structure of a bacterial cell as revealed by electron microscopy. (London, part of question)

5   Discuss the sources, effects and control of pollution in the atmosphere. (London, S)

6   Outline the functions of each of the following organelles:
(a) Golgi apparatus,
(b) microtubules,
(c) ribosomes,
(d) nucleolus. (London)

7   Compare and contrast the carbon and nitrogen cycles.
(UCLES, S)

# chapter 2

# Proteins

The Swedish chemist Berzelius realised the importance of proteins when he gave them their name in 1838: the word 'protein' comes from the Greek '*proteios*', which means 'first'. Even simple organisms such as *Escherichia coli* have about 1000 different types of protein molecule in their cells. For humans, the number is probably between 50 000 and 100 000. Most of these proteins are enzymes; for every step in a biochemical reaction, there is a specific enzyme catalyst. But proteins carry out other tasks, particularly in complex organisms such as ourselves. Some of these are listed in Table 2.1.

It is the overall shape of a protein that is the key to its functioning. This shape depends upon chemical bonding within the molecule.

**Table 2.1   Some of the functions of proteins in the human body**

| Protein | Function |
| --- | --- |
| Haemoglobin | transport of oxygen |
| Actin | muscle contraction |
| Collagen | strengthens skin and bone |
| Immunoglobulins (antibodies) | immune protection |
| Rhodopsin | receptor for light stimuli |
| Nerve growth factor | formation of neural networks |

## 2.1   Amino acids are the building blocks of proteins

Proteins are polymers. Their relative molecular masses range from 5500 to 220 000. Molecular masses are sometimes measured in daltons, after John Dalton, who developed the atomic theory of matter. Haemoglobin, for example, has a molecular mass of 68 000 daltons, or 68 kilodaltons (kd), and a *relative* molecular mass of 68 000. The recently discovered protein dystrophin (which is absent or malfunctioning in the inherited disease muscular dystrophy) has a molecular mass of 350 000 daltons, and is probably the largest protein known.

The building blocks of proteins are amino acids (Figure 2.1). These are molecules that contain a hydrogen atom, a **carboxyl** group and an **amino** group bonded to a carbon atom known as the **α carbon** atom (α = alpha). The fourth group – labelled R in Figure 2.1 – differs in each amino acid. There are 20 naturally occurring amino acids, as shown in Table 2.2. They are divided into four different types, **acidic**, **basic**, **polar** and **non-polar**, depending on the chemical nature of their R group. Polar groups have an affinity for water, whereas non-polar do not (see also the Appendix on basic chemistry). The ionic charge on an amino acid depends upon pH. At low pH, the amino group accepts a proton (hydrogen ion or $H^+$), giving an overall positive charge; while at high pH, the carboxyl group loses a proton ($H^+$), leading to a negative charge on the molecule (Figure 2.2).

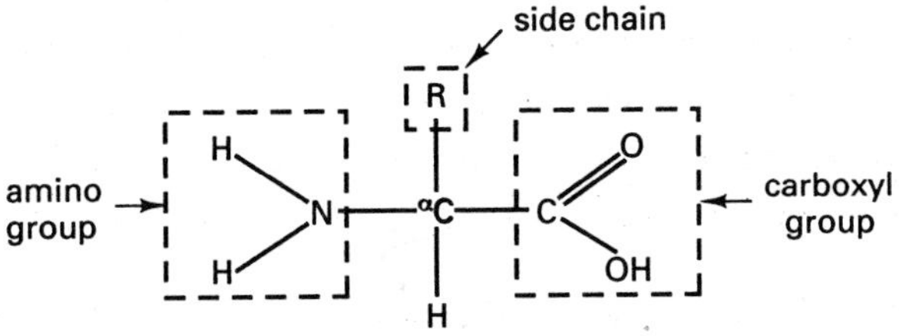

Figure 2.1
General
formula of an
amino acid.

**Table 2.2    The amino acids in proteins (N = non-polar, P = polar, A = acidic, B = basic)**

| Amino acid | Abbreviation | Code | R group | Type |
|---|---|---|---|---|
| Alanine | Ala | A | $- CH_3$ | N |
| Arginine | Arg | R | $- (CH_2)_3 - NH - C {\nwarrow}^{NH}_{NH_2}$ | B |
| Asparagine | Asn | N | $- CH_2 - CO - NH_2$ | P |
| Aspartic acid | Asp | D | $- CH_2 - COOH$ | A |
| Cysteine | Cys | C | $- CH_2 - SH$ | P |
| Glutamine | Gln | Q | $- (CH_2)_2 - CO - NH_2$ | P |
| Glutamic acid | Glu | E | $- (CH_2)_2 - COOH$ | A |
| Glycine | Gly | G | $- H$ | N |
| Histidine | His | H | $- CH_2$ 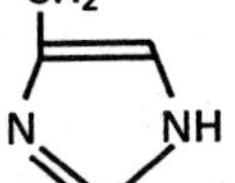 (imidazole ring with N, NH, H) | B |
| Isoleucine | Ile | I | $- C {\atop CH_3}^{H} - C_2H_5$ | N |

(*continued p.28*)

| Leucine | Leu | L | 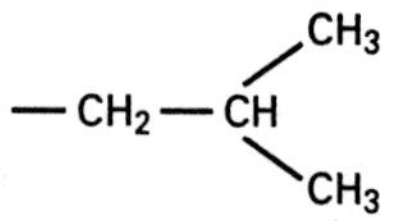 $-CH_2-CH\begin{smallmatrix}CH_3\\CH_3\end{smallmatrix}$ | N |
| Lysine | Lys | K | $-(CH_2)_4-NH_2$ | B |
| Methionine | Met | M | $-(CH_2)_2-S-CH_3$ | N |
| Phenylalanine | Phe | F | 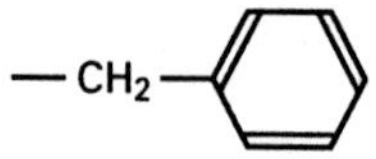 $-CH_2-\bigcirc$ | N |
| Proline | Pro | P | 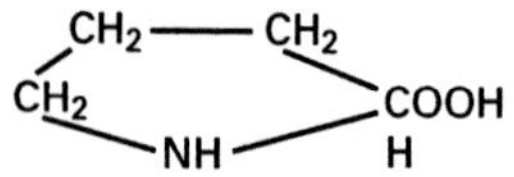 $CH_2\underset{NH}{\overset{CH_2---CH_2}{\diagdown}}\overset{COOH}{\underset{H}{}}$ (structure of whole molecule) | N |
| Serine | Ser | S | $-CH_2-OH$ | P |
| Threonine | Thr | T | $-C\underset{H}{\overset{OH}{|}}-CH_3$ | P |
| Tryptophan | Trp | W | 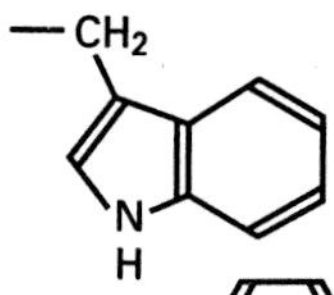 $-CH_2$ | N |
| Tyrosine | Tyr | Y | 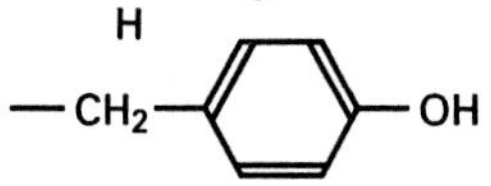 $-CH_2-\bigcirc-OH$ | P |
| Valine | Val | V | 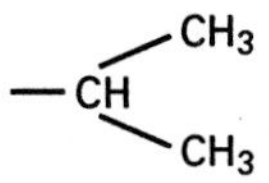 $-CH\begin{smallmatrix}CH_3\\CH_3\end{smallmatrix}$ | N |

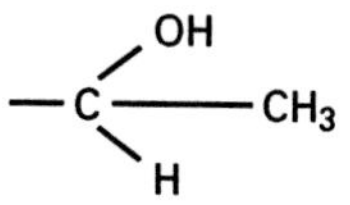

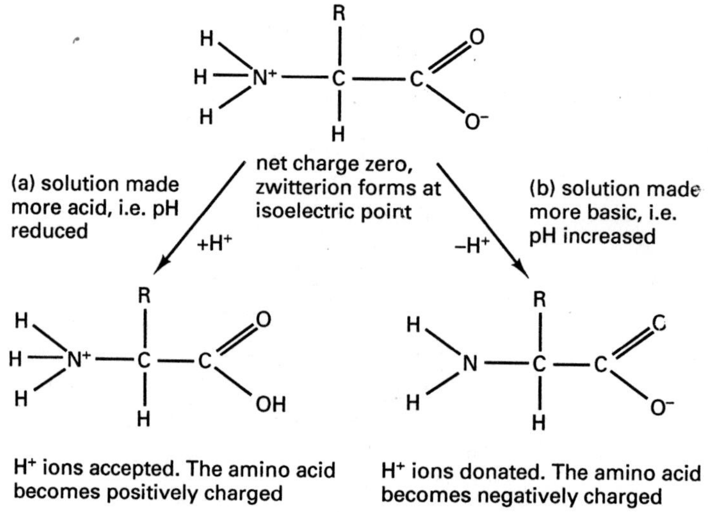

Figure 2.2
Effect of (a)
acid and (b)
alkali on an
amino acid.

net charge zero, zwitterion forms at isoelectric point

(a) solution made more acid, i.e. pH reduced

$+H^+$

(b) solution made more basic, i.e. pH increased

$-H^+$

H$^+$ ions accepted. The amino acid becomes positively charged

H$^+$ ions donated. The amino acid becomes negatively charged

Between the extremes, there is a pH value called the **isoelectric point** at which the positive charge on the amino group just balances the negative charge on the carboxyl group. When the molecule is in this form, it is called a **zwitterion** and has no *net* charge.

## The peptide bond

Two amino acids can join together when the amino group of one reacts with the carboxyl group of another in a condensation reaction. A **peptide bond** is formed, and the product is called a **dipeptide** (Figure 2.3a). When many amino acids condense together in this way, the result is a **polypeptide chain** (Figure 2.3b) or protein. Polypeptides of length greater than 100 amino acid residues are classed as proteins, while shorter ones are called peptides. Polypeptides usually contain between 50 and 2000 amino acids. Amino acids in a peptide chain are often called **residues**.

In the late 1930s two American chemists, Linus Pauling and Robert Corey, began a detailed study of the structures of polypeptides. One of the first things

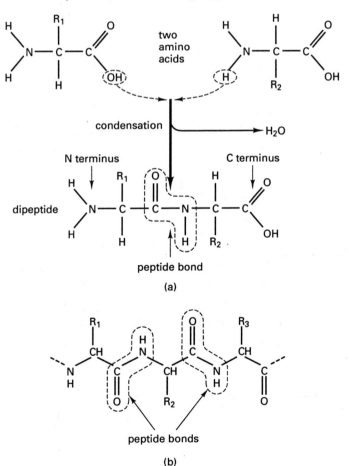

Figure 2.3 (a) Formation of a dipeptide by condensation of two amino acids. (b) Part of a polypeptide chain.

they discovered was that the peptide groups were always flat and rigid, while
the rest of the polypeptide chain was fairly flexible. This helps the protein
molecule to keep its shape.

QUESTION    **1 The average relative molecular mass of an amino acid is 100. How many
amino acids does dystrophin contain?**

## Primary structure

The amino acid units in a polypeptide chain are known as residues and they are
usually written down in the three- or one-letter codes given in Table 2.2. By
convention, the residue with the free amino group is written on the left, and is
known as the N-terminus, while the residue with the free carboxyl group on
the right is called the C-terminus.

Most proteins contain cysteine residues. Cysteine contains sulphur atoms,
which can form bonds with the sulphur atoms of other cysteine residues
elsewhere in the protein molecule. These S–S bonds are known as **disulphide
bridges.** Sometimes they join two or more polypeptide chains together in a
protein.

The primary structure of a polypeptide is the sequence of amino acids in its
polymer chain. The correct sequence can be crucial to the protein's function.
Just one mistake in a protein can lead to serious disease. For instance, compare
the following sequences of two people for a segment of the protein, Factor IX,
that helps the blood to clot:

Ser-Trp-Gly-Glu-Glu-Cys-Ala-Met-Lys-Gly-Lys-Tyr-Gly-Ile-Tyr

Ser-Trp-Gly-Glu-Glu-Tyr-Ala-Met-Lys-Gly-Lys-Tyr-Gly-Ile-Tyr

The top sequence belongs to a healthy person, while the bottom one belongs
to a man suffering from a severe form of haemophilia.

QUESTION    **2 What are the symptoms of haemophilia? What is the molecular defect
that causes the disease in the above case?**

## Amino acid analysis

The first step in determining the primary structure of a protein is to find out the
type and number of amino acids that it contains. This is called amino acid
analysis. The protein is hydrolysed with concentrated hydrochloric acid at
$100\,°C$ for 24 hours in a sealed, evacuated tube. This chemical treatment breaks
all the peptide bonds, leaving a mixture of free amino acids known as a **protein
hydrolysate.**

Before they can be identified, the amino acids in the hydrolysate are
separated from each other by a technique called **ion-exchange chromatography.** A sample of hydrolysate is applied to the top of a stainless-steel column

containing an ion-exchange resin. The resin consists of polystyrene molecules chemically linked to sulphonate groups, which have a negative charge.

The sulphonate groups attract positive charges on the amino acids, so that the protein hydrolysate binds to the resin. Buffer mixtures of increasing pH are then pumped through the column and the amino acids are washed off the column one at a time. Aspartic acid, which binds most weakly to the column, comes off first. The last one to emerge is arginine, because it sticks onto the resin more firmly than do the other amino acids (Figure 2.4).

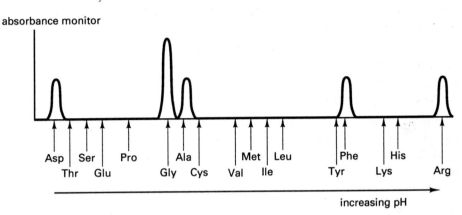

Figure 2.4
Elution profile
of protein
hydrolysate (a
hexapeptide
containing
Asp, Gly, Ala,
Phe, Arg).

The separated amino acids are then treated with ninhydrin to give a purple compound. The colour intensity of each one is measured by a colorimeter to give its concentration. Figure 2.4 shows an example of the type of amino acid profile that emerges from the colorimeter; this is a paper trace from a recorder that responds to changes in absorbance.

The absorbance of each peak is proportional to its colour intensity, which in turn depends upon how much amino acid it contains. Figure 2.4 shows a trace from a protein hydrolysate that contains twice as many glycine residues as alanine residues (from the relative size of their absorbance peaks). We know where to find the individual amino acids on the profile because the amino acid analyser has been **calibrated**; each amino acid is run through the instrument separately before work on the analysis of proteins begins, and its position on the trace noted for future reference. The data from the trace in Figure 2.4 are processed by a computer to give the amino acid composition of the protein (see Figure 2.5).

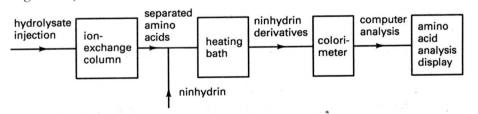

Figure 2.5
Block diagram
of fully
automated
amino acid
analyser.

**3 Write down three possible amino acid sequences for the hexapeptide (i.e. made up of six amino acids) whose profile is given in Figure 2.4.**     QUESTION

## Protein sequencing

The longer a polypeptide chain becomes, the larger the number of possible sequences. Amino acid analysis gives no information about the sequence of a protein. This is deduced by Edman degradation, the chemistry of which is shown in Figure 2.6.

**Figure 2.6**

**Edman**

**degradation**

**(one cycle).**

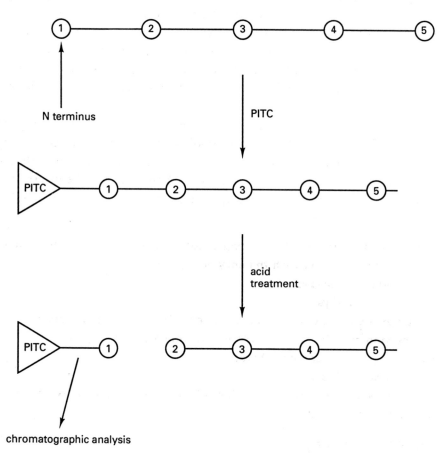

First, the N-terminus reacts with a chemical tag called phenylisothiocyanate (PITC). In the next step, acid cleaves the PITC-labelled amino acid from the protein and the cycle starts again. Meanwhile, the PITC-labelled amino acid passes into a chromatographic system for analysis. This consists of a separating column and a recorder similar to the one described above for amino acid analysis. The main differences are that generally an absorbent material other than an ion-exchange resin is used to pack the column, and there is no need for reaction with ninhydrin. The data are processed, again, by computer and the sequence is displayed on a screen. The procedure is now fully automated – all the scientist has to do is to load a protein sample into the instrument and the first residue will be identified within about two hours.

**4 Draw a block diagram similar to Figure 2.5 to show how an automated protein sequencer works.**   QUESTION

In practice, a complete protein sequence cannot be obtained by Edman degradation, because the process becomes inefficient after about 50 residues. Sometimes, just knowing the first few residues at the N-terminal end of the protein is enough to identify it. The rest of the sequence can be obtained by scanning a protein database such as the one at the European Molecular Biology Laboratory in Heidelberg, which is available to research laboratories all over the world.

However, when a new protein has been isolated, then the complete sequence will be required. One way of finding this is to chop the protein up into manageable fragments with an enzyme. These peptide fragments are separated by chromatography. The sequence of each can then be determined by Edman degradation. The entire sequence can probably be pieced together as in the following example.

**5 The following two peptides (among others) were obtained when a small protein was incubated with the enzyme trypsin:**   QUESTION
**(a) Ala-Ala-Trp-Gly-Lys**
**(b) Thr-Asn-Val-Lys**
**Draw out the two possible sequences for this region of the protein.**
**A second experiment, with the enzyme chymotrypsin, gave the following peptide (among others):**
**(c) Val-Lys-Ala-Ala-Trp**
**This was called the 'overlap' peptide. What is the correct sequence for this region of the protein?**

## Frederick Sanger

Fred Sanger won a Nobel Prize in 1958 for his work on protein sequencing. He pioneered the development of **end-group analysis** using 2,4-dinitrofluorobenzene (DNFB) as a chemical tag for the N-terminus. Amino acids tagged with DNFB turn yellow. After hydrolysis, only the N-terminal amino acid carries the yellow marker. Analysis of the protein hydrolysate identifies this amino acid.

Sanger chose to work on insulin, which, with a relative molecular mass of 6000, is a fairly small protein. Insulin is a hormone that controls the use of sugar in the body. Initially, Sanger worked on beef insulin, which contains 51 amino acid residues. End-group analysis quickly showed that there are two polypeptide chains in the insulin molecule (Figure 2.7).

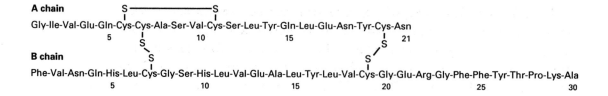

**A chain**

S————————————S
|                           |
Gly-Ile-Val-Glu-Gln-Cys-Cys-Ala-Ser-Val-Cys-Ser-Leu-Tyr-Gln-Leu-Glu-Asn-Tyr-Cys-Asn
        5    S      10       15      S  21
           S

**B chain**           S                         S

Phe-Val-Asn-Gln-His-Leu-Cys-Gly-Ser-His-Leu-Val-Glu-Ala-Leu-Tyr-Leu-Val-Cys-Gly-Glu-Arg-Gly-Phe-Phe-Tyr-Thr-Pro-Lys-Ala
        5         10         15         20         25         30

**Figure 2.7**
**Amino acid**
**sequence of**
**beef insulin.**

Sanger then set to work analysing and sequencing these two chains by partial hydrolysis in which the weakest peptide links were broken. It took him and his co-workers a year of painstaking work on each fragment to reveal the structure of just one of the polypeptide chains (this was long before automatic sequencers were developed). More research was then needed to find out how the two chains are linked in the insulin molecule.

News of Sanger's sequencing technique spread fast. The American chemist Vincent du Vigneaud attracted the attention of the Nobel Prize Committee with his sequencing of the two small peptides oxytocin and vasopressin. These are nonapeptide (nine amino acid) hormones produced by the pituitary gland at the base of the brain. Vasopressin regulates water balance, while oxytocin controls lactation. Chemically they are very similar. Du Vigneaud proved the correctness of his work by synthesising both peptides from their component amino acids, a technique that is common among organic chemists trying to confirm the structures of natural products.

Sanger's work was of great significance to the early molecular biologists such as Jacques Monod and Francis Crick. The insulin sequence had demonstrated, for the first time, that proteins consist of an amino acid sequence for which there are no obvious chemical rules. For example, we cannot say 'glycine always follows tyrosine'. For Monod and Crick this confirmed their suspicions that some kind of code was needed for the synthesis of proteins by the cell.

**QUESTION**  **6 Oxytocin has the following amino acid sequence:**
**Gly-Leu-Pro-Cys-Asn-Gln-Ile-Tyr-Cys**
**Write a detailed plan of how you would attempt to confirm its primary structure.**

## Fingerprinting

The analysis of abnormal proteins in certain diseases can lead to a firm diagnosis and greater understanding of the illness. The most famous example of this was in 1954, when Vernon Ingram used a technique called **fingerprinting** to pinpoint the exact molecular differences between normal haemoglobin and the abnormal haemoglobin in the blood of people suffering from **sickle cell anaemia** (SCA).

In SCA, about 50 per cent of the red blood cells take up a crescent or sickle shape, which causes them to block the blood vessels, leading to circulatory problems, and kidney and heart failure. The abnormal red blood cells are also more fragile than normal ones, and have a shorter lifetime, which leads to severe anaemia. The cause of the sickling is precipitation of the abnormal haemoglobin within the red blood cell. SCA is an **autosomal recessive disease**. This means that the gene involved is located on a chromosome other than the X (sex) chromosome, and that people suffering from the disease are homozygotes, with two faulty alleles. Heterozygotes – with one normal and one faulty allele – have sickle cell trait and usually show no symptoms. Around 1 per cent of their red blood cells are sickled.

In Ingram's analysis of SCA, haemoglobin samples were first treated with enzymes to give a mixture of peptides. These were then separated by a two-dimensional process. The first separation was by paper **electrophoresis**. This works by loading the sample onto paper soaked in buffer. An electric field is then applied to the paper. The peptides have an ionic charge, and so move through the electric field at a speed that depends upon their size.

The paper is then turned through 90° and the peptides are separated further by chromatography (Figure 2.8). The result is a 'fingerprint' of the protein. Ingram showed that one of the peptides differed in position between normal and sickle cell haemoglobin.

Amino acid analysis of this peptide showed that the faulty protein had a valine residue in place of a glutamic acid residue. This alone was able to account for all the physiological signs and symptoms of sickle cell anaemia, and set the scene for the analysis of molecular defects in inherited disease.

**Figure 2.8**

**Fingerprinting.**

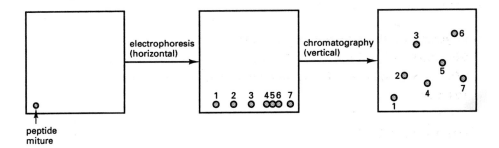

peptide
miture

**2.2**  ## Secondary structure accounts for the properties of fibrous proteins

The simple linear polypeptide sequences given in the last section are useful for displaying primary structure, but proteins never exist in this form in the cell. Instead, hydrogen bonds form between the CO and NH groups of the polypeptide chain (sometimes known as the **backbone** of the protein), resulting in two types of secondary structure – the **α-helix** and the **β-pleated sheet**. These structures were suggested by Pauling and Corey from their work with molecular models of amino acids. They are responsible for the properties of the fibrous proteins that give strength to silk, feathers, bone and hair.

### The α-helix

In an α-helix, the polypeptide chain is twisted into a spiral shape and is held in place by hydrogen bonds between CO groups and NH groups, which have three complete residues between them (Figure 2.9). So each turn of the helix contains 3.6 residues.

**Figure 2.9 The α-helix (straight lines are hydrogen bonds).**

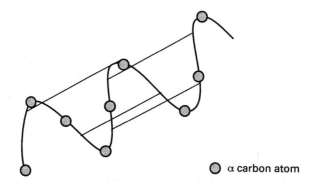

⦿ α carbon atom

α-Helices can coil around each other to form long filaments. These are found in **α-keratin**, the main component of wool and hair, where a triple coil is held together by disulphide bridges. Myosin and tropomyosin in muscle fibres, and fibrin in blood clots, form similar coiled structures. Another form of α-keratin accounts for the hardness of beaks and claws. Instead of forming individual coils, the helices in the protein lie side by side in sheets, joined by disulphide bridges. The sheets are stacked on top of each other, held together with more disulphide bridges. This gives a very hard, strong structure.

QUESTION  **7 Pauling used a simple paper chain model to demonstrate the α-helix. Simulate this by drawing out a section of poly(glycine) on a long strip of paper. Now model it into the shape of Figure 2.9, and check the length of the hydrogen bonds. Would helices with two or four amino acids between the hydrogen bonds be stable?**

## The β-pleated sheet

In the β-pleated sheet, neighbouring polypeptide chains are linked together by hydrogen bonds to give a ridged sheet-like structure (Figure 2.10). The chains can be running in the same (parallel) or opposite (anti-parallel) directions.

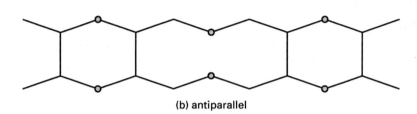

(a) parallel

◎ α carbon atom

(b) antiparallel

Figure 2.10 The β-pleated sheet (vertical lines are hydrogen bonds).

Silk, a solidified fluid excreted by silkworms and spiders, is another type of keratin, **β-keratin**. It has a β-pleated sheet structure. This means that, unlike wool or hair, silk cannot be stretched easily because the polypeptide chains are already fully extended. The sheets are stacked on top of each other, held loosely in place by hydrogen bonds. Silk is flexible because these sheets slide over one another easily.

**QUESTION**    8 Tortoiseshell and silk are both made from keratin. Account for the differences in their properties in terms of protein structure.

## Collagen

Collagen holds you together; it is a component of skin, bone, blood vessels and teeth. It is found in all multicellular organisms, and makes up a quarter of the body mass of mammals. It is the longest protein known and consists of a triple helix. However, these are not α-helices. Collagen contains a high proportion of both proline and glycine. In fact, every third residue is glycine – an unusual regularity in a protein sequence. The proline residues twist out of each other's way, forming the helices, while the glycine, being small, allows the close approach of the three helices to form the collagen molecule (Figure 2.11). The helices are held together by hydrogen bonding between the NH groups of glycine and the CO groups of the next chain.

The importance of the glycine is underlined in the disease **osteogenesis imperfecta**. In this inherited disorder, severe deformities resulting from

Figure 2.11 The triple helix of collagen.

multiple fractures are common in early childhood. This happens because the collagen structure is not formed properly, leading to brittle bones. Recent research shows that the collagen defect is the substitution of just one glycine in the whole molecule by a cysteine residue.

## Proteins at the hairdresser's

The α-keratin in hair forms coils in which three helices are wound round one another and held in place by disulphide bonds. These coils cluster together in groups of 11 to form microfibrils. Bundles of hundreds of microfibrils stack together to give a single hair (Figure 2.12).

Shampoos and conditioners cause pH changes that affect the hair by altering the ionic charge on the protein molecules. This can make the coils tighter, which results in the reflection of more light, making the hair look shiny. It can also make individual hairs repel one another, giving the hair more 'body'.

The disulphide bridges are affected by some of the chemicals used at the hairdresser's because cysteine is prone to oxidation and reduction. Hydrogen

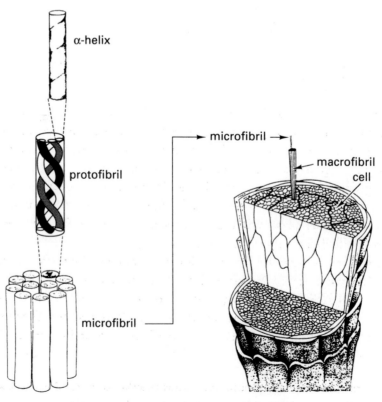

**Figure 2.12 The structure of a hair.**

α-helix

protofibril

microfibril

microfibril

macrofibril cell

hair fibre

peroxide, which is used to bleach the hair, oxidises cysteine in the keratin, making more disulphide bridges as it removes hydrogen atoms connected to the sulphur. This leaves the hair brittle. Perming lotion has the opposite effect – breaking disulphide bonds. The helices are unwound as the hair is styled, and then the disulphide bonds are re-formed by the neutralising solution, leading to a 'permanent wave'.

**9 Why is it not advisable to have hair bleached and permed at the same time?**    QUESTION

 ## Tertiary structure accounts for the properties of globular proteins, including enzymes

Unlike fibrous proteins, globular proteins have a compact, roughly spherical shape. They have regions of secondary structure, but are folded into an overall tertiary structure. Enzymes are globular proteins, as are transport proteins such as myoglobin and haemoglobin.

The tertiary structure is held together by four types of chemical bonds as listed below:

- disulphide bridges
- hydrogen bonds
- salt bridges
- hydrophobic bonds

Although hydrogen bonds can be formed between atoms on the main polypeptide chain, bonds made between the side chains of the residues are also important in tertiary structure (Figure 2.13). **Salt bridges**, for example, are made between acidic and basic side chains with negative and positive charges such as those of glutamic acid and lysine. These bonds are similar to those which hold together the sodium and chloride ions in common salt. **Hydrophobic bonds** occur between hydrocarbon side chains of non-polar amino acids, such as valine and leucine.

This means that residues that are widely separated in the protein sequence may be close together when it is folded into its tertiary structure. Polar side chains tend to face outwards, towards an aqueous solvent, while non-polar side chains are buried in the protein core. As a result, the polar side chains can hydrogen bond with water, meaning that globular proteins are soluble in water.

**10 Using Table 2.2 list the amino acids that would be more likely to be found (a) on the surface and (b) in the core of a protein.**    QUESTION

Figure 2.13
Computer-
generated
picture of the
tertiary
structure of
trypsin (the
atoms are
unlabelled).

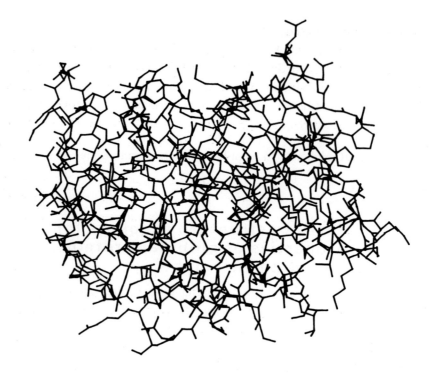

The tertiary structures of proteins are usually determined by **X-ray crystallography**. To date, about 200 protein structures have been determined in this way. Advances in protein sequencing mean that there are now thousands of proteins with known primary structures waiting for their tertiary structures to be determined.

However, analysis of these sequences with computer databases has shown that proteins tend to occur in families. For example, the digestive enzymes, trypsin and chymotrypsin, as well as the blood-clotting protein, thrombin, are all in the family known as the **serine proteases**. Computer models can be built of proteins in the same family if the structure of just one of them has already been determined by X-ray crystallography.

Computer graphics has largely replaced manual model-building as a way of displaying the structures of big proteins. The latter is difficult and time-consuming, and there is also the danger that such a model may collapse under its own weight! A computer image of a protein can be magnified and rotated, and the effect of making changes in the protein sequence can be tried out. These methods are now used extensively by pharmaceutical companies to design new, more effective, drugs by visualising how these will interact with target protein molecules. This approach, which saves a great deal of laboratory time and effort, has been used to model how antibiotics attack bacterial proteins and to explore the action of peptide hormones such as vasopressin.

## X-ray crystallography

X-ray crystallography was developed by the father-and-son team of William and Lawrence Bragg between 1912 and 1915. It was first used to investigate the internal structure of simple crystalline substances such as sodium chloride. In X-ray crystallography a beam of X-rays is shone through a crystalline specimen. As it passes through, it interacts with the electrons around each atom in the crystal and is deflected from its original direction. The transmitted beam falls onto a film sensitive to X-rays and forms a pattern of spots, which is characteristic of the way the beam has been scattered by the atoms of the crystal. This pattern is determined by the spacing of atoms in the crystal; it contains all the information needed about the arrangement of atoms (or ions) in the crystal. The first X-ray pictures of simple substances were easy to interpret.

The potential of the method for biological molecules such as proteins was first realised in the 1930s when J. D. Bernal and Dorothy Hodgkin, working in Cambridge, obtained X-ray photographs of the digestive enzyme, pepsin. They were, at this stage, unable to interpret their results, because basic structural features such as the α-helix had not at that time been put forward. However, they continued to collect data.

Myoglobin, an iron-containing protein that carries oxygen in muscle, was the first protein whose tertiary structure was solved by X-ray crystallography

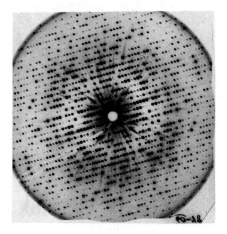

**Figure 2.14 The tertiary structure of myoglobin: X-ray photograph.**

(Figure 2.14). This was the result of pioneering work done by John Kendrew and Max Perutz at Cambridge University and was published in 1958. The next year saw the determination of the structure of haemoglobin, a more complex protein, which Perutz had been working on for nearly 30 years. He and Kendrew were rewarded with the Nobel Prize for their efforts in 1962.

**11 Explain the difference in the information given about a protein from amino acid sequencing and X-ray crystallography.**   QUESTION

## 2.4   Quaternary structure

Some proteins contain more than one polypeptide chain. Each one is called a **subunit**. The way in which subunits are linked together is called the **quaternary structure**. Haemoglobin, for example, has four subunits – one pair called the α-subunits and one pair called the β-subunits (Figure 2.15). Each has a different amino acid sequence. All four subunits link to a molecule called haem, which gives blood its red colour and contains an iron atom. Haemoglobin carries oxygen around the body. The subunits fit together in a way that allows the molecule to contract when oxygen binds to it, and to expand again when the oxygen is released to the cells. This 'breathing' motion of haemoglobin is made possible by its quaternary structure.

The haem in haemoglobin is an example of a **prosthetic group**. This is a non-protein molecule to which the protein must be conjugated to function biologically. Other prosthetic groups include carbohydrates and metal ions.

**Figure 2.15 The structure of haemoglobin.**

$\beta_2$     $\beta_1$

$\alpha_2$     $\alpha_1$

## 2.5   Proteins are denatured by heat and pH changes

If the network of bonds that hold together the tertiary structure of a protein is disrupted, biological activity is lost. This change is called **denaturation** and can be brought about by heat or pH changes.

Heat energy breaks hydrogen bonds. Many proteins are denatured by temperatures above 50 °C. Strong acid or alkali alters the charges on amino acid side chains, breaking up salt bridges. Solutions of high salt concentration have a similar effect. Detergents tend to disrupt hydrophobic bonds.

Denaturation may be temporary or permanent. Spontaneous refolding of a protein from its linear structure – **renaturation** – is possible under certain conditions.

## Proteins in the kitchen

The high protein content of eggs and meat leads to interesting changes of texture when they are cooked. For instance, egg-white proteins denature on whisking; the long polypeptide chains tangle together, or **coagulate**, trapping air to form a liquid foam, which may have up to eight times the volume of the original mixture. Adding sugar to make meringue, and then baking the mixture, causes further expansion. Meringue is an excellent insulator, because of the large amount of air it contains. If a block of ice cream is smothered in meringue and cooked very rapidly (three minutes) on the hottest oven setting, you have the pudding 'Baked Alaska'; the ice cream stays frozen because it is insulated from the heat of the oven by the meringue.

When an egg is boiled, the egg-white proteins denature and coagulate at a lower temperature than the egg-yolk proteins. So three minutes boiling produces a runny yolk and a solid white. The soft texture of scrambled egg is produced by a coagulated protein mesh that traps water. Too much cooking produces a leathery texture as the mesh thickens and squeezes out the trapped water.

Meat is the muscle tissue of animals. It consists of muscle fibres, which contain the proteins actin and myosin, held together by connective tissue, which contains collagen. When meat is cooked, actin and myosin denature and coagulate. If cooking is overdone, the meat becomes tough. But collagen softens when it is heated, which makes the meat moist and tender. For a successful Sunday roast, the meat must be cooked long enough to let the collagen denature, but not so long that the muscle proteins over-coagulate.

### 2.6　Peptides and proteins have many uses

Aspartame (Nutrasweet™) is a dipeptide with the following formula:

Asp-Phe

It is widely used as a sweetener in products such as soft drinks and yoghurts. Aspartame is 200 times sweeter than sucrose and is useful for slimmers – a diet yoghurt sweetened with aspartame has about a quarter of the calories of one with added sugar. However, like other peptides, it breaks down on heating, so cannot be used in baked goods such as cakes.

Some peptide hormones are used as drugs. For example, many diabetics depend on a daily dose of insulin. Formerly this was extracted from pig pancreas. It is now made in bacteria by genetic engineering.

Proteins also have many applications. The uses of enzymes will be considered in Chapter 9. Apart from enzymes, the main uses of proteins are concerned with the immune system. Briefly, the immune system in animals works by producing large proteins known as **antibodies** or **immunoglobulins** from **lymphocyte** cells in response to the presence of a foreign molecule called an **antigen**. Many antigens are themselves proteins, and the principle of vaccination depends upon injecting antigens to stimulate the production of protective antibodies.

The original vaccines were killed versions or weaker versions of the infecting organism. Some, like the whooping cough vaccine, were 'dirty' or contaminated with bacterial toxins. Although many of the original vaccines are still in use, there is a move towards using pure antigenic proteins, or even peptide fragments of these, as vaccines.

## Monoclonal antibodies

An antibody recognises and binds to regions known as **epitopes** on an antigen's surface. Animals have a very large range of lymphocytes, each of which produces a different antibody to the antigen. These antibodies differ from each other in their affinity and specificity for different epitopes. So a single antigen typically produces a mixture of antibodies known as a **polyclonal antibody**. However, in a cancer known as **multiple myeloma**, one type of lymphocyte begins to divide uncontrollably, producing large amounts of a single immunoglobulin. Such antibodies are called **monoclonal antibodies**, because they come from a single population of lymphocytes.

**Figure 2.16**
**Production of**
**monoclonal**
**antibodies.**

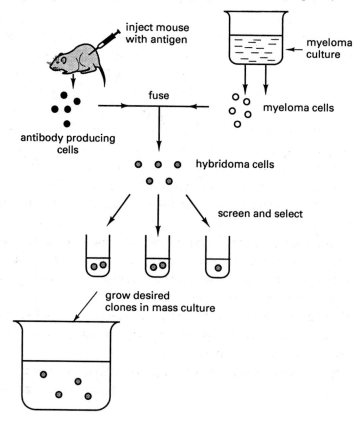

Normal lymphocytes do not live for more than a few days in culture. However, in 1975, Georges Kohler and Cesar Milstein showed that, if the lymphocytes were fused to myeloma cells, it was possible to produce large amounts of monoclonal antibodies in culture (Figure 2.16).

Because they bind proteins (the antigens from which they were originally derived) with a known specificity and affinity, monoclonal antibodies have many applications. They can be used to extract proteins from blood plasma, leading to a pure protein product. They are also useful in diagnosis, because they bind to enzymes in clinical samples and can be used to detect them. Monoclonal antibodies can also be used to deliver cytotoxic drugs to cancer cells because they recognise and bind to carbohydrates on the surface of these cells (Figure 2.16).

## Summary of Chapter 2

1. Proteins are polymers made up of small molecules called amino acids. There are 20 common amino acids, of four kinds – basic, acidic, polar and non-polar. Their state of ionisation depends upon pH.

2. The primary sequence of an amino acid gives the order of amino acids in the polypeptide chain. This can be determined by chemical methods.

3. Proteins have secondary and tertiary structures, which determine their overall shape. There are two important types of secondary structure – the α-helix and the β-pleated sheet. Secondary structure is important in determining the properties of fibrous proteins.

4. Globular proteins depend upon their tertiary structure for their function. Four types of chemical bond are important in determining tertiary structure – hydrogen bonds, disulphide bridges, salt bridges and hydrophobic bonds. The nature of the tertiary structure is determined by the side chains in the protein's sequence.

5. Quaternary structure is important for some proteins and describes the way subunits of the protein fit together. Some proteins are conjugated to prosthetic groups – non-protein molecules that are needed for the protein's biological activity.

6. Proteins are denatured by heat, extremes of pH and detergents, which cause them to lose the tertiary structure on which their biological activity depends.

7. Peptides and proteins have a variety of uses in industry and in medicine.

## Examination questions

Figure 2.17

Amino acid P                    Amino acid Q

1   Figure 2.17 shows the structural formulae of two amino acids P
    and Q.
    (a) Name two elements, other than carbon, hydrogen and
        oxygen, which may be present in groups $R_1$ and $R_2$.
    (b) P and Q may be linked during protein synthesis. In this
        reaction certain atoms from P and Q combine to form new
        molecules.
        (i) Copy the diagram and draw a circle around the atoms
            that are removed when P and Q are linked together.
        (ii) Draw a line connecting the atoms in P and Q that are
            bonded together.
        (iii) Name the bond formed by this reaction.
    (c) Explain how the different properties of groups such as $R_1$ and
        $R_2$ are important in the structure and functioning of proteins.
        (London)

2   (a)   (i) Describe the structure of proteins.
          (ii) State briefly how globular proteins differ from fibrous
              proteins and give an example of where each may be
              found.
    (b) Describe how specific factors that affect enzyme activity do so
        by their action on the protein component of enzymes. (JMB,
        now NEAB, A/S)

3   On partial hydrolysis, a peptide with five amino acids gave a
    mixture of the following:
    qp, qs, rq, qsq
    [where p, q, r and s represent four different amino acids]. What is
    the sequence (a) qprqs, (b) qsqpr, (c) rqpqs, (d) rqsqp? (JMB, now
    NEAB, A/S)

4   State what is meant by each of the following terms: (a) peptide
    linkage, (b) conjugated protein. (London, part of question)

# chapter 3

# Nucleic acids

The nucleus is the control centre of the cell, directing the synthesis and activities of proteins. It also acts as the cell's 'library', storing vital information about protein sequences in a chemical database. Nucleic acids are the chemical units that carry out these functions. As with proteins, a knowledge of the chemical structure of these molecules is the key to understanding how they work.

## 3.1   DNA is life's blueprint

Just as a building is constructed from an architect's blueprint, so living things also work to a plan. This plan is contained in chemical units called **genes**, which are long stretches of a polymer called **DNA (deoxyribonucleic acid)**.

In eukaryotes, DNA is located in the cell nucleus, in thread-like structures called **chromosomes**, which can be seen under a light (optical) microscope if the appropriate stain is used. In prokaryotes, the DNA lies free in the cytoplasm. The total of the DNA in an organism is known as its **genome**.

DNA is also found in mitochondria and chloroplasts. This suggests that these organelles may once have been free-living organisms, each with its own set of genes. According to the theory of **endosymbiosis**, these organisms could have set up mutually beneficial associations with eukaryotes during the course of evolution. Cyanobacteria, with their photosynthetic apparatus, could have been absorbed into a eukaryotic partner, which gave it some protection against the Earth's changing climate. The partnership eventually evolved into a higher plant, with the cyanobacteria developing into a chloroplast but still retaining its own DNA and separate membrane.

DNA contains all the information needed for the synthesis of proteins, including their sequences, as a chemical code. Understanding the chemical basis of genetics through the study of DNA has probably been the most significant step forward in the history of biology.

### The transforming principle

Proteins have a complex chemical structure, while DNA is (relatively) simple. For many years these facts misled scientists about the importance of DNA. Most were convinced that it had to be the proteins in the chromosomes that carried genetic information – because they were complicated. Then, in 1928,

Fred Griffith, a microbiologist at the Ministry of Health in London, did some experiments that gave puzzling results. He was working with strains of *Pneumococcus* bacteria. One type could cause pneumonia, and because it gave smooth colonies when grown in a Petri dish it was called S type. Another type was harmless, because it lacked the sugar (or polysaccharide) coating that gave the S-type colonies their smooth appearance and helped them to evade the body's natural defences. The harmless pneumococci were called R type – they gave rough colonies on Petri dishes.

Griffith showed that heat treatment killed the S-type pneumococci and made them harmless. To his surprise, however, he found that if he injected mice with a mixture of live R and dead S bacteria, the mice died, and he found live S pneumococci in their blood. Biologists who realised the importance of Griffith's work began to say that a substance called the 'transforming principle' had passed from the dead S to the live R bacteria. This caused the bacteria to change their genetic nature or **genotype** and enabled them to make the polysaccharide coat normally found in the S strain.

But what was the transforming principle? In 1944, after ten years of careful investigation, Oswald Avery and his team at the Rockefeller Institute, New York, showed that the transforming principle is DNA. DNA on it own could make R cells become virulent. Avery's work was backed up by experiments carried out by Alfred Hershey and Martha Chase in 1952 using **bacteriophages** (viruses that infect bacteria). Hershey and Chase exploited one of the chemical differences between DNA and protein for their experiment. Only DNA contains phosphorus, while only protein contains sulphur. The bacteriophage DNA was tagged with a radioactive phosphorus label and their protein coat with a radioactive sulphur label. The radioactive bacteriophage was then allowed to infect *Escherichia coli*. Hershey and Chase then used a food blender to break open the bacteria and find out what was inside them. The cells contained radioactive phosphorus, showing that DNA, not protein, had passed into the cells. DNA was Griffith's 'transforming principle'.

**QUESTION**  1 How could Griffith have used Hershey and Chase's radioactive labels to confirm that his 'transforming principle' was DNA?

### 3.2  Nucleic acids are polymers

The other important nucleic acid is **RNA (ribonucleic acid)**. There are actually three types of RNA. **Ribosomal RNA** is the main component of ribosomes, **transfer RNA** is found in the cytoplasm, while **messenger RNA**, as its name suggests, shuttles between the nucleus and the ribosome. RNA is involved in protein synthesis. DNA and RNA are also the main component of viruses. The human immunodeficiency virus (HIV), which causes AIDS, is an RNA virus.

The nucleic acids are polymers whose basic unit is known as a **nucleotide**.

Only four types of nucleotide occur in DNA and RNA, which means that they are chemically less complex than the proteins. However, they are very long molecules – one molecule of *E. coli* DNA, for example, has a length of about 1 mm, while the diameter of one of its proteins would be about 10 nm.

A nucleotide consists of three components: a **base**, a **sugar** and a **phosphate** group (Figure 3.1). There are five different bases. Three of them, **thymine**, **uracil** and **cytosine** (usually abbreviated to T, U and C), belong to the chemical family known as the **pyrimidines**, while the other two, **adenine** and **guanine** (A and G), belong to the purine family. There are two sugars, **ribose** and **deoxyribose**, which differ by only one oxygen atom, found in nucleotides.

As its chemical name suggests, DNA has deoxyribose as its sugar. It also

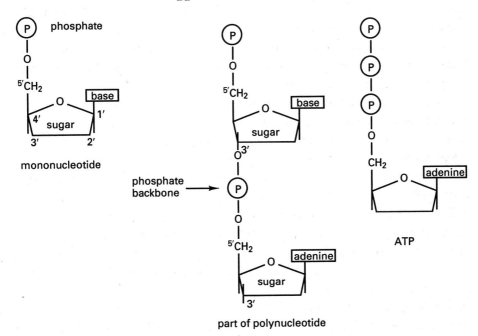

Figure 3.1
Structure of
nucleotides.

has the bases A, T, C and G – making four possible types of nucleotide in its sequence. RNA is very similar, but has ribose instead of deoxyribose and U instead of T.

The nucleotides are linked together through their phosphate groups, which are the 'backbone' of the polynucleotide molecule (Figure 3.1). The end with the free phosphate group is called the 5′ end and the other is the 3′ end. The order in which the bases are arranged in the polynucleotide is known as its **sequence**. The longer a DNA molecule is, the more possibilities there are for different sequences of the four bases. The entire sequence of human DNA contains about $3 \times 10^9$ bases. The base content of DNA differs between organisms.

The chemical formula of DNA is not enough, on its own, to tell us how it works in the cell. We also need to know how the DNA molecule is arranged in space – its three-dimensional structure. In the 1950s three groups of scientists were working on this key problem. Linus Pauling, in the United States, had the advantage of being an expert on chemical bonding. He had also worked on the structure of proteins. In London, Rosalind Franklin and Maurice Wilkins were looking at the X-ray crystallographic pictures of DNA. But the structure eluded all three, leaving two unknowns in the field – James Watson and Francis Crick of Cambridge University – to solve the puzzle with a mixture of luck, persistence and model building.

They worked out that a double helical structure, with two strands of DNA wound around one another, would fit the X-ray data, but they knew that any structure they proposed would have to explain Chargaff's rules. The Austrian chemist Erwin Chargaff had analysed DNA from many different organisms. His results are shown in Table 3.1. Chargaff's data showed that the purine content (A+G) was always equal to the pyrimidine content (C+T). Furthermore, the amount of A equals the amount of T, which means that the amounts of C and G are also equal.

**Table 3.1   Percentage of the different bases in DNA from different organisms (molar amounts)**

| Source of DNA | A | G | T | C |
|---|---|---|---|---|
| Human | 30.9 | 19.9 | 29.4 | 19.8 |
| Sheep | 29.3 | 21.4 | 28.3 | 21.0 |
| Hen | 28.8 | 20.5 | 29.2 | 21.5 |
| Turtle | 29.7 | 22.0 | 27.9 | 21.3 |
| Salmon | 29.7 | 20.8 | 29.1 | 20.4 |
| Sea urchin | 32.8 | 17.7 | 32.1 | 17.3 |
| Locust | 29.3 | 20.5 | 29.3 | 20.7 |
| Wheat | 27.3 | 22.7 | 27.1 | 22.8 |
| Yeast | 31.3 | 18.7 | 32.9 | 17.1 |
| *E. coli* | 24.7 | 26.0 | 23.6 | 25.7 |
| $\Phi \times 174$ (bacteriophage) | 24.6 | 24.1 | 32.7 | 18.5 |

The essential feature of Crick and Watson's final model is base-pairing. They cut out cardboard models of the four bases and, as they were puzzling over how to fit them together, hydrogen bonding expert Jerry Donohue happened to visit the laboratory. He showed them how hydrogen bonds could link the four bases into two pairs: A + T and C + G (Figure 3.2).

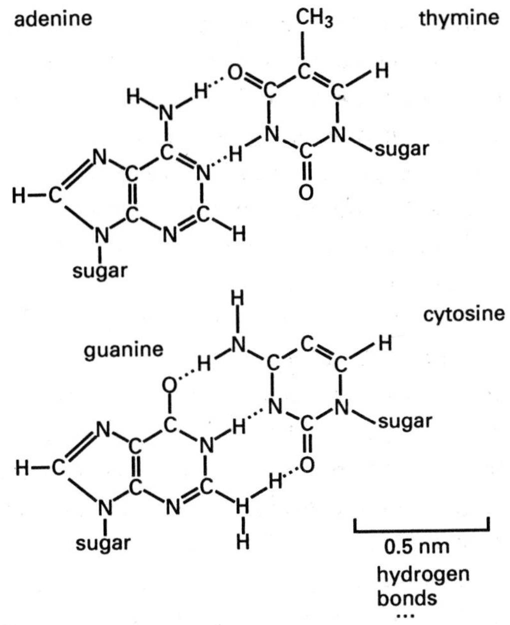

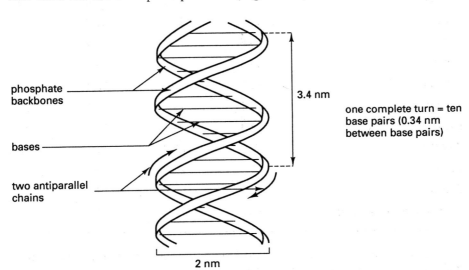

adenine                    CH₃        thymine

sugar

H—C

sugar

Figure 3.2
Adenine–
thymine and
guanine–
cytosine base
pairs.

cytosine

guanine

H—C

sugar

0.5 nm
hydrogen
bonds
...

Then the rest of the model fell into place. Two anti-parallel DNA molecules are wound around one another in a double helical strand. The phosphates are on the outside and the bases face each other on the inside, held in pairs by hydrogen bonds. A complete turn of the double helix is 3.4 nm long and there are ten base pairs per turn (Figure 3.3).

Figure 3.3
Diagrammatic
structure of
DNA.

phosphate
backbones

3.4 nm

one complete turn = ten
base pairs (0.34 nm
between base pairs)

bases

two antiparallel
chains

2 nm

**2 Use the information in this section to work out the length of a human DNA molecule.**

QUESTION

## Rosalind Franklin

In 1962, Crick, Watson and Wilkins received the Nobel Prize for their work on DNA. Tragically, Rosalind Franklin died of cancer in 1958 at the early age of 37, and the Nobel Prize is never awarded posthumously. Watson wrote a book *The Double Helix* about the 'race' for the DNA structure in which he comments that Franklin and Wilkins had a poor working relationship. However, Maurice Wilkins was a close friend of both Watson and Crick and showed Watson one of Franklin's X-ray photographs, without her knowledge. In Watson's own words, 'The instant I saw the picture, my mouth fell open and my heart began to race.' The information in this picture undoubtedly helped him and Crick to put together the final, correct DNA model.

Rosalind Franklin was a superb experimentalist, who pioneered the use of X-ray crystallography to explore the structures of biological molecules. She continued to work on the structures of viruses right up to her death.

 **Eukaryotic DNA is tightly packed inside the nucleus**

The length of a DNA molecule is usually measured in base pairs (bp) or thousands of base pairs (**kilobases** or kb). Table 3.2 shows the lengths of DNA molecules in different organisms.

**Table 3.2  Lengths of DNA molecules**

| Organism | Base pairs/kb | Length/µm |
|---|---|---|
| *Vaccinia* virus | 190 | 65 |
| *E. coli* | 4000 | 1360 |
| Yeast | 13 500 | 4600 |
| *Drosophila* (fruit fly) | 165 000 | 56 000 |
| Human | 2 900 000 | 990 000 |

The two ends of the *E. coli* DNA molecule are joined together to form a loop. To fit into the bacterial cell, the molecule is tightly coiled. A eukaryotic chromosome contains a single linear DNA molecule, tightly bound to small protein molecules called **histones**. Histones contain many basic lysine residues. The positive charges on the lysine side chains form strong ionic bonds with the phosphate backbone of DNA, which is negatively charged.

The DNA molecule winds itself around groups of eight histones, forming a bead-like structure called a **nucleosome**. The nucleosomes themselves are wound into a solenoid. Further looping and coiling of the solenoids around non-histone scaffolding proteins completes the packing of DNA into chromosomal form (Figure 3.4).

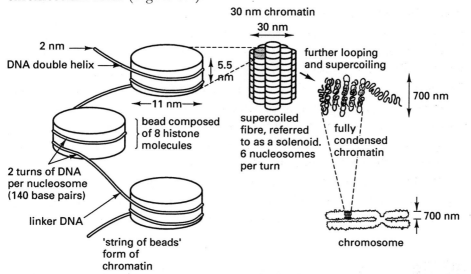

Figure 3.4 Proposed structure of the nucleosome and its relationship to the chromosome and the DNA molecule.

# 3.4 DNA copies itself

When cells divide, a copy of the DNA from the original cell must be transferred to any new cells that are formed, because its sequence is the database that the cell needs to function. Before mitosis or meiosis, DNA copies itself so that the chromosomes are already doubled up before the nucleus divides.

It is the chemical structure of DNA that drives the copying mechanism. Although they did not know the details, Crick and Watson hinted at this in their famous 1953 paper in the journal *Nature*, which first described the DNA double helix. They wrote, 'It has not escaped our notice that the specific pairing we have postulated immediately suggests a possible copying mechanism for the genetic material.'

In 1958, American biochemists Mathew Meselsohn and Franklin Stahl carried out an experiment that suggests how DNA copies itself or replicates. First, they grew some *E. coli* in a medium that was normal in every way except that it contained ammonium chloride labelled with $^{15}N$, a heavy isotope of nitrogen. The bacteria built up their DNA from this medium and the bases contained 'heavy' nitrogen instead of the normal isotope, $^{14}N$. Then Meselsohn and Stahl transferred the bacteria into a normal medium, containing $^{14}N$. After one generation, they harvested the bacteria and extracted DNA from them. They already knew that DNA containing $^{15}N$ could be distinguished from DNA containing $^{14}N$ by a technique known as **density gradient centrifugation**. When the mixture is suspended in a solution of caesium chloride and whirled round at high speed in a centrifuge, two distinct

Figure 3.5
Replication of
the DNA
double helix.

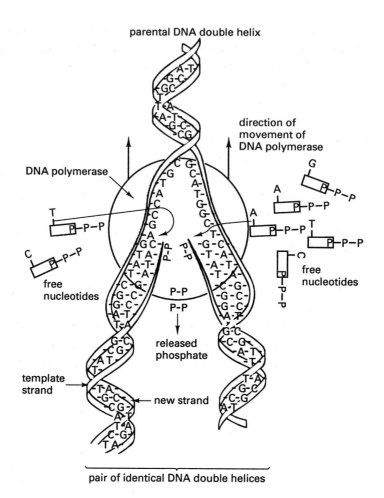

pair of identical DNA double helices

bands of DNA form in the tube, well separated from each other. The heavier DNA is found lower down the tube than the lighter DNA. Their positions are detected by the absorption of ultraviolet light.

The DNA from the first round of replication gave a band that occurred in a position exactly mid-way between those of $^{14}$N DNA and $^{15}$N DNA. This result supports the idea of semi-conservative replication (see Figure 3.5). First, DNA unwinds into two single strands as the weak hydrogen bonds break under the influence of the enzyme **DNA polymerase**. The single strands then attract individual nucleotides, which line up next to their complementary bases (i.e. A with T, G with C). The enzyme **DNA ligase** then joins up the phosphate backbone on the new strand. Synthesis takes place from the 5′ to the 3′ end. This new pair contains one strand from the original pair and a new strand – hence the name **semi-conservative replication**. In Meselsohn and Stahl's experiment, the original strand contained $^{15}$N and the new strand contained $^{14}$N. This hybrid strand gave rise to the DNA band mid-way between $^{14}$N DNA and $^{15}$N DNA.

3 Suppose DNA replication was conservative, with copying taking place on double-stranded rather than on single-stranded DNA. Predict the types and amounts of DNA that Meselsohn and Stahl would have observed after (a) one cycle and (b) three cycles.

4 What happens to DNA when it is heated?

## The polymerase chain reaction

Kary Mullis of the Cetus Corporation in California was driving along a freeway (motorway) in 1985, when he suddenly had the idea that was to revolutionise DNA research. Mullis was lucky: the first time he tried out his experiment, it worked! Now the **polymerase chain reaction** (PCR) is used in laboratories all over the world to multiply DNA – creating billions of copies of each molecule in a tiny sample.

The PCR (Figure 3.6) is based on the way DNA is multiplied in the cell. A sample of DNA containing a sequence of interest is heated to separate the strands. At the same time, a supply of free nucleotides is added to the mixture, along with short, synthetic DNA sequences called **primers**. These act as markers, because they bind to the sequence at its beginning and end. As the mixture cools, the primers move into position. If a polymerase enzyme is now

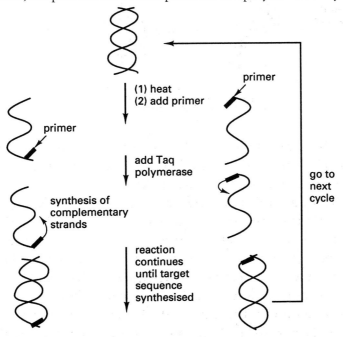

Figure 3.6 The polymerase chain reaction.

added, it will run up and down the single strands, assembling the new chains. So now two copies have been produced from the original one. If the cycle is repeated, there will be four copies, then eight and so on. The process is **exponential**, doubling the number of copies on each turn of the cycle. After 30 hours, more than a billion copies will have been produced from each molecule.

In the early days of PCR, the only drawback was that, each time the DNA was heated, it denatured the polymerase enzyme. This meant that time and money were wasted in adding fresh enzyme during each cycle. Then Mullis had another idea. He began to use a polymerase from *Thermophilus aquaticus*, a bacterium that lives in hot springs. **Taq polymerase**, as it is called, is heat-stable and can be used over and over again without being destroyed in the heating step. This means that PCR is now fully automated. The uses of PCR include prenatal diagnosis of inherited disease, the analysis of forensic samples and the extraction of DNA from mummies and mammoths in the new science of 'molecular archaeology'.

QUESTIONS   **5 What would be the sequence of the primer you would need to amplify a DNA sequence beginning CTAAAGCTCTGGAGA?**

**6 You start off with a microgram (1 μg) of DNA from a blood sample. How much is there after ten cycles of the PCR?**

## Summary of Chapter 3

1   DNA controls the activities of proteins in the cell. It also contains information about the proteins in the form of units called genes. DNA, not protein, is therefore the genetic material.

2   The three types of RNA play an important role in protein synthesis. DNA and RNA are nucleic acids. They are both polymers built from nucleotides. The nucleotides themselves consist of a phosphate group, a sugar and a base linked together.

3   DNA has a double helix structure in which the two strands are held together by base-pairing. In base-pairing the bases adenine and thymine hydrogen bond to each other, as do cytosine and guanine to each other. DNA is packed into chromosomes in eukaryotes by association with histone proteins, but it lies in a free loop in the cytoplasm of prokaryotes.

4   DNA undergoes semi-conservative replication every time a cell divides. This is controlled by the enzymes DNA polymerase and DNA ligase. It involves unwinding of the DNA double strands followed by synthesis of complementary strands.

## Examination questions

1   Review the experiments and observations which enable the statement to be made that DNA molecules are the basis of heredity in virtually all living things. (IB, Subsidiary Level)

2   Figure 3.7 represents part of the molecular structure of a nucleic acid.

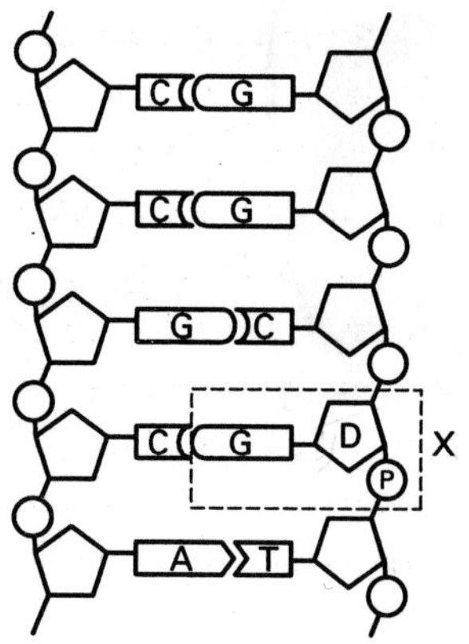

(a) (i) Where in a eukaryotic cell would you expect to find it?
   (ii) Name the part of the molecule inside the dotted line labelled X in the diagram.
   (iii) What do the letters C, D, P and T represent?

Figure 3.7

(b) Biochemical analysis of a sample of DNA showed that 33 per cent of the nitrogenous bases was guanine. Calculate the percentage of the bases in the sample which would be adenine. Show your working. (London)

3 Bacteria were grown for several generations in a medium containing the heavy isotope of nitrogen $^{15}N$ and were then transferred to a medium containing the normal isotope $^{14}N$. Samples were taken after the bacteria had completed one, two and then three divisions. DNA was extracted from the bacteria at each stage in the process and analysed using the technique of density centrifugation. The DNA was measured by means of its absorption of ultraviolet wavelengths. The results of this experiment are shown below.

Figure 3.8

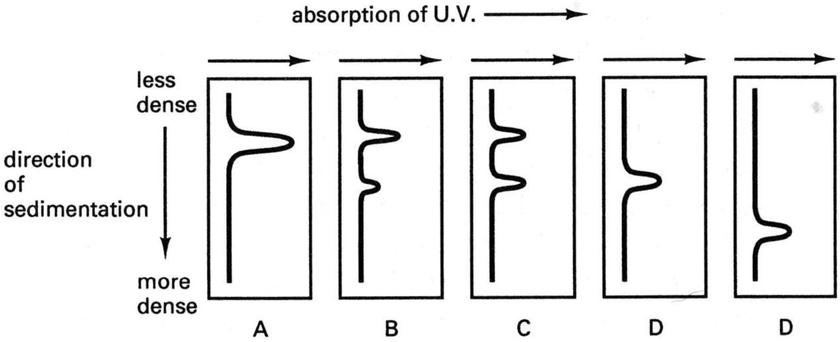

For each of the bacteria treatments described below give the letter of the appropriate density gradient profile of the extracted DNA:

(a) the first generation after the bacteria grown in $^{15}N$ medium were transferred to $^{14}N$ medium;
(b) the second generation after transfer;
(c) the third generation after transfer;
(d) bacteria grown for several generations in the $^{15}N$ medium.
   (JMB, now NEAB)

# chapter 4

# Lipids and cell membranes

The lipids are a large group of naturally occurring substances that are characterised by their insolubility in water. They have a wide variety of chemical structures and play a number of roles in living organisms. They include fats and oils, hormones and the components of cell membranes.

## 4.1 Fats, oils and waxes contain fatty acids

Most fat and oil molecules are built upon a **glycerol** backbone, in which the three alcohol groups have been replaced by long-chain **fatty acids** (Figure 4.1) in an esterification reaction. Fats and oils are also known as triglycerides because of this chemical structure.

**Figure 4.1**
Formation of a lipid by condensation of glycerol with fatty acids.

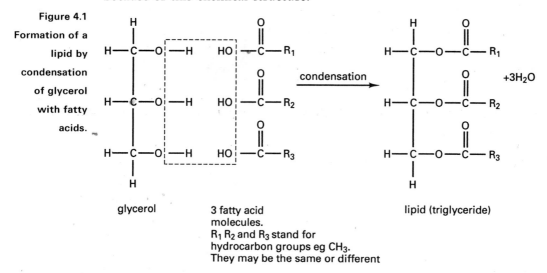

glycerol

3 fatty acid molecules.
$R_1$ $R_2$ and $R_3$ stand for hydrocarbon groups eg $CH_3$.
They may be the same or different

lipid (triglyceride)

The fatty acids contain a carboxyl group linked to a hydrocarbon chain. The long hydrocarbon chains are **hydrophobic** – they dislike water – and it is their presence in fats and oils that makes them insoluble.

Fats and oils fall into two categories – **saturated** and **unsaturated** – depending on the type of fatty acid they contain. Saturated fatty acids contain only single bonds in their hydrocarbon chain, while mono-unsaturated and poly-unsaturated fatty acids have one or more than one double bond respectively. Some examples are given in Table 4.1.

**Table 4.1   Types and occurrence of some fats and oils**

| Name of acid | Type | Occurrence |
| --- | --- | --- |
| Stearic | saturated | chocolate |
| Palmitic | saturated | beef fat |
| Oleic | mono-unsaturated | olive oil |
| Linoleic | poly-unsaturated | corn and rapeseed oils |
| Clupanodonic | poly-unsaturated | cod liver oil |

Unsaturated fatty acids have lower melting points than saturated fatty acids. Organisms that are well adapted to low temperatures such as fish and certain plants have high proportions of unsaturated fatty acids in their lipids.

Fats and oils tend to be mixtures, with a broad melting or boiling range. An exception is cocoa butter, the main component of chocolate, which has a fairly uniform fat composition. Its melting point is about 34°C, just below body temperature. This is why chocolate melts in the mouth. The melting process produces a cooling effect, which is part of the taste sensation of chocolate.

**1 Which of the fatty acids listed in Table 4.1 would you expect to find in (a) soap and (b) sunflower oil?**          QUESTION

## Energy storage and protection

Triglycerides are good energy storage compounds because of their insolubility and the fact that they release more energy than carbohydrates when they are broken down – about $38\,kJ\,g^{-1}$ compared to about $17\,kJ\,g^{-1}$. **Glycogen**, the carbohydrate energy store, is hydrated in the cell, binding about twice its own mass of water by hydrogen bonding, while fats and oils repel water. When hydration is taken into account, nearly 7 g of glycogen are needed to give the same energy as 1 g of triglyceride. For an average human, replacing triglyceride energy reserves with glycogen would almost double her or his body mass.

Triglycerides are stored in specialised fat, or **adipose**, cells and are broken down into fatty acids and glycerol by enzymes known as **lipases**. Fatty acids can produce a great deal of ATP – for example, one molecule of palmitic acid produces 129 molecules of ATP when it is broken down.

Plants store oils, many of which are important in the human diet, in their seeds. There is an increasing interest in exploiting these plant oils, such as castor oil, as an alternative to petroleum to manufacture plastics, detergents and cosmetics.

Fats are good insulators. Animals such as whales, Antarctic seals and penguins living in cold climates have extensive fatty layers beneath their skin, which protect against loss of body heat.

Waxes are not triglycerides. They are formed from the esterification of a fatty acid and a long-chain alcohol and are solids at room temperature. They are found as a protective layer on fruits, leaves, skin and insect cuticles. They make a useful waterproof barrier because of their insolubility, and protect the organism from dehydration.

**QUESTION**    **2 The World Health Organisation (WHO) recommends that fat should make up 15–30 per cent of our daily energy intake. In the UK, it is about 38 per cent. The change could be made by eating less fat and more carbohydrate. The average daily intake of fat in the UK is about 130 g. By how many grams should this be reduced to reach the upper limit of the WHO guidelines? Estimate how many more grams of carbohydrate you would have to eat to make up the difference in energy intake.**

### 4.2    Cholesterol is an important lipid in animal cells

**Cholesterol** is one of a group of lipids known as the **steroids**. Steroids have a characteristic chemical structure consisting of 17 carbon atoms joined together in a set of five- and six-carbon rings (Figure 4.2). In the 1940s, Konrad Bloch showed that rats fed with radio-labelled acetate (ethanoate) – a compound with only two carbon atoms – produced cholesterol in which each of the 27 carbon atoms was radio-labelled. In later years, biochemists were able to work out exactly how acetate assembles itself into the ring structure of cholesterol. Such chemical processes, where complex molecules are built up from simple building blocks in the cell, are an example of **biosynthesis**. Cholesterol biosynthesis in mammals occurs mainly in the liver. Some foods, such as eggs and cream, are concentrated sources of cholesterol in the diet.

Cholesterol is an important component of animal cell membranes and a biosynthetic precursor for other lipids such as the sex hormones and vitamin D. However, excess cholesterol in body fluids leads to deposits on artery walls known as **atherosclerotic plaques**. These can block blood flow, leading to heart attacks and strokes. This condition, known as **atherosclerosis**, is a major cause of death in the Western world.

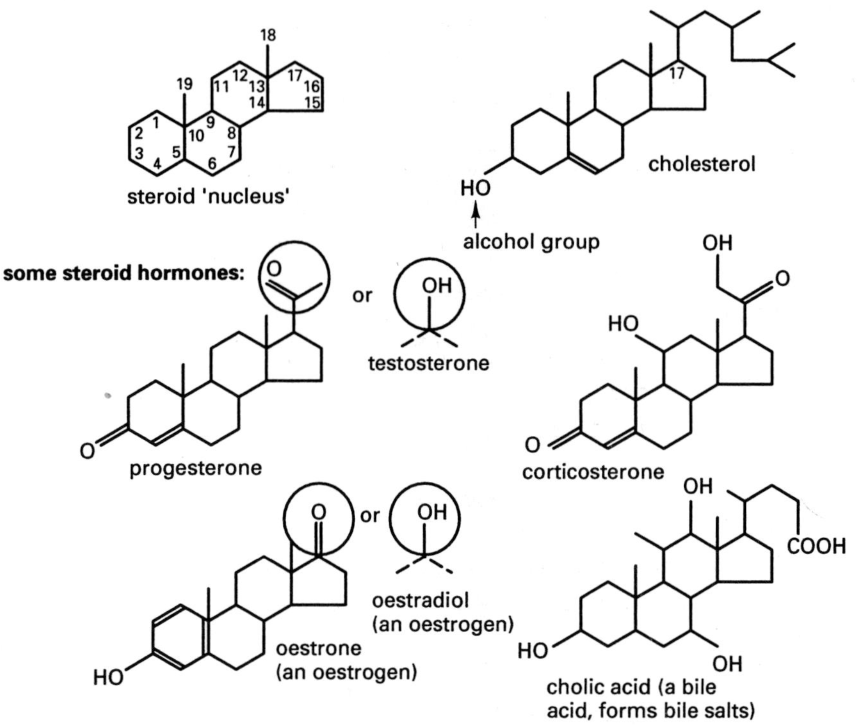
18
19
11
12
13
14
17
16
15
1
2
3
4
5
10
9
8
7
6
steroid 'nucleus'
17
cholesterol
HO
alcohol group
some steroid hormones:
O
or
OH
testosterone
OH
O
HO
O
progesterone
O
corticosterone
O
or
OH
oestradiol
(an oestrogen)
OH
COOH
oestrone
(an oestrogen)
HO
HO
OH
cholic acid (a bile
acid, forms bile salts)

**Figure 4.2** Structures of steroids.

## Controlling cholesterol levels

It is obviously important to keep the amount of cholesterol in the body at the right level. The liver helps to control cholesterol levels by cutting back on biosynthesis in response to the presence of dietary cholesterol. The other way in which the body stops blood cholesterol from building up is to move it quickly from the blood into the cells.

Lipids such as cholesterol are carried around the body in particles known as **lipoproteins**. This overcomes the transport problem caused by the insolubility of lipids. A lipoprotein consists of a lipid core embedded in a protein coat. The main cholesterol carrier in the blood is called **low-density lipoprotein** (LDL) (Figure 4.3).

The outside surfaces of cell membranes are studded with proteins called LDL receptors. These hook onto circulating LDLs and pull them inside the cell. Here they are dismantled, and the cholesterol is released.

The importance of LDL receptors was shown by studies of an inherited disease known as **familial hypercholesterolaemia** (FH). FH is characterised by very high levels of cholesterol in plasma – between 300 and 680 mg $l^{-1}$, compared to a normal level of 175 mg $l^{-1}$. Those patients with a very high level tend to die of heart disease at an early age. Severe cases can be treated by liver transplant, but a more common therapy is to give drugs that lower cholesterol levels.

**Figure 4.3
Model of
low-density
lipoprotein.**

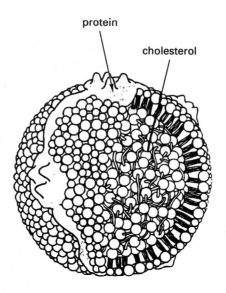

protein

cholesterol

It has been shown that the molecular defect in FH is in the LDL receptor. Either the receptor is absent completely, or it does not function correctly because of a defect in the protein's structure.

QUESTION    3 Why do you think atherosclerosis is such a major killer in industrialised countries? What public health measures could be adopted to improve this situation?

### 4.3    Cholesterol is the source of many lipids

Further biosynthesis leads to the formation of a number of steroid hormones from cholesterol (see Figure 4.2). These are synthesised in a number of different organs in the body. For instance, glucocorticoids and mineralocorticoids are hormones synthesised in the adrenal glands, while the female and male sex hormones are made in the ovary and testes respectively.

The female sex hormones are **oestrogen** and **progesterone**. Oestrogen is responsible for the development of secondary sexual characteristics, as well as for regulation of ovulation. Progesterone prepares the uterus for implantation and is involved in the maintenance of pregnancy. The androgens – of which **testosterone** is the main one – are responsible for male secondary sexual characteristics.

Synthetic sex hormones can be used in a number of ways: the contraceptive pill is a mixture of hormones that simulates a state of pregnancy and suppresses ovulation. The menopause can be suppressed by giving oestrogen – many doctors say that this prevents bone loss (**osteoporosis**) in later life.

The **glucocorticoids** and the **mineralocorticoids** are involved in glycogen formation and regulation of blood pressure respectively. Bile salts are made in the liver and are the main constituent of bile. These polar compounds act like detergents. They break up dietary lipids into tiny particles, increasing their surface area. This enables lipases to break them up more effectively, and also helps their absorption into the intestine.

**Vitamin D** is present in few natural foods – an exception is fish liver oils – and must be synthesised in the body. It is important in calcium and phosphate metabolism. Its synthesis from cholesterol requires ultraviolet light, however. The effects of lack of sunlight can be seen in the development of the bone softening known as **rickets** (in children) and **osteomalacia** (in adults). Rickets was once common in English children, before the importance of fortifying foods such as milk with vitamin D was realised. Osteomalacia has been recorded in Bedouin Arab women, who traditionally cover themselves completely, except for their eyes.

**4 Why is the transport of cholesterol around the body so important?**      QUESTION

### 4.4   Phospholipids can organise themselves into bilayers

**Phospholipids** are molecules that are built upon a backbone of either glycerol or a more complex alcohol called sphingosine. In the phosphoglycerides, which are based on glycerol, two of the hydroxyl groups are attached to fatty acids, but the third is bound to a phosphate group (Figure 4.4).

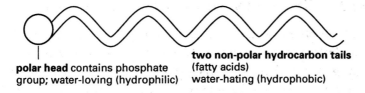

**polar head** contains phosphate group; water-loving (hydrophilic)

**two non-polar hydrocarbon tails** (fatty acids) water-hating (hydrophobic)

Figure 4.4 Simplified representation of a phospholipid molecule.

The phosphoglycerides differ from the triglycerides in having one group that is dissimilar in its properties to the other two. The phosphate group is hydrophilic, while the hydrocarbon chains of the fatty acid groups are hydrophobic. In a phosphoglyceride molecule, the two fatty acid groups line up together, attracted by hydrophobic forces (similar to those which help to give a protein its tertiary structure). The hydrophilic phosphate group points in the opposite direction.

When phospholipids are mixed with water, they can arrange themselves into two types of structure – **micelles** or **bilayers** (Figure 4.5). Micelles are globular structures in which the hydrophobic ends cluster together in a central core, while the hydrophilic tails point outwards, facing the aqueous solvent. Micelles are more often found in detergent molecules such as soap rather than phospholipids. (Soap is a sodium salt of a fatty acid such as stearic acid and also has a hydrophilic and hydrophobic end.)

The plasma membranes that surround cells are made up of phospholipid bilayers. These membranes have been studied using **erythrocyte ghosts**. When red blood cells are placed in water, the salt concentration inside the cell is greater than that of its surroundings. This causes water to pass into the cell by **osmosis** (the movement of water from a region of low to high solute), causing them to swell and burst, leaving only the membrane behind. Analysis shows that the erythrocyte membrane is 40 per cent lipid and 60 per cent protein and carbohydrate. In other membranes the ratio of lipid to protein varies. Membranes are also found inside cells where they separate organelles such as mitochondria from the cytoplasm.

**Figure 4.5**
**Phospholipids form organised structures.**

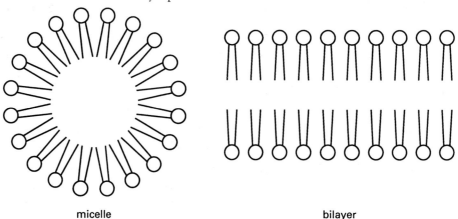

micelle                    bilayer

The lipid bilayer in a cell membrane is not a rigid sheet. The individual lipid molecules can move sideways (laterally) in their layer. For example, a lipid molecule in a bacterial membrane has been shown to move from one end of the bacterium to the other in just one second. The lateral movement of lipids in a membrane is controlled, in prokaryotes, by the chemical composition of the fatty acid in the lipids. In eukaryotes, this control is exerted by cholesterol molecules, which are embedded, at intervals, in the membrane structure. These molecules form a barrier to the lateral movement of the lipids. This model of the membrane is known as the **fluid mosaic model** (Figure 4.6).

QUESTION   **5 Look at Figure 4.6 overleaf and describe how the inner and outer surfaces of the cell membrane differ. Where would you locate the LDL receptor? How many different kinds of protein are there in the cell membrane?**

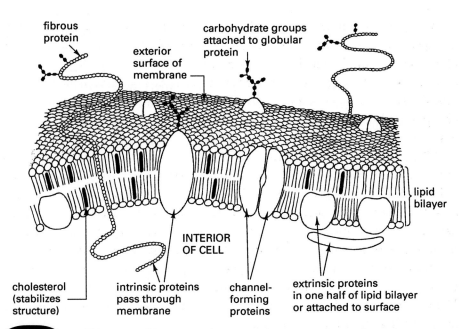

fibrous protein

carbohydrate groups attached to globular protein

exterior surface of membrane

lipid bilayer

INTERIOR OF CELL

cholesterol (stabilizes structure)

intrinsic proteins pass through membrane

channel-forming proteins

extrinsic proteins in one half of lipid bilayer or attached to surface

Figure 4.6 Fluid mosaic model of plasma membrane structure.

## 4.5    The cell membrane is a selective barrier

The cell membrane separates the cell from its environment but also allows materials in and out. The high lipid content of the membrane means that it has a low permeability to ions and polar molecules, with the exception of water, which passes in and out relatively easily.

Some substances move through the membrane by **diffusion**. Diffusion is a spontaneous process that allows molecules to travel down a concentration gradient – always from high to low concentrations. Diffusion may be assisted by allowing the molecules to pass through channels in the bilayer rather than through the bilayer itself. These channels are long crevices in protein molecules embedded in the membrane. Some of the channels possess molecular flaps, which are open or closed depending on the exact chemical environment of the cell. These gated channels are particularly important in the transport of ions through nerve cell membranes.

Sometimes substances have to move against a concentration gradient. This is known as **active transport** and requires the expenditure of energy on the part of the cell. Pumps driven by ATP are available in the membrane to assist in active transport. Again, these pumps consist of proteins embedded in the lipid bilayer.

Some of these proteins are **glycoproteins**, tagged with carbohydrate groups. The carbohydrates are always located on the outer cell surface, because they are hydrophilic, where they play a role in intercellular recognition. They help cells to organise themselves into tissues, and act as labels for the cell that can be detected by the immune system of other organisms (or sometimes even by the same organism).

## Cystic fibrosis results from a defective membrane protein

**Cystic fibrosis** (CF) is one of the commonest inherited diseases in the Western world, affecting 1 in 2000 people. Its symptoms include repeated and severe lung infections, which drastically reduce life expectancy. The discovery in 1989 of the faulty gene that leads to CF opened the way to understanding the cause of the disease, which is the first step to more effective treatment.

CF patients have sweat that is saltier than normal, suggesting a problem with the transport of sodium chloride through cell membranes. This was confirmed in the early 1980s when researchers showed that the cell membranes of CF sufferers were impermeable to chloride ions.

More seriously, CF causes the excretion of very sticky mucus from the cells lining the lungs. This means that there is also a problem with the transport of water through the membrane. The mucus is a breeding ground for infection. Intensive daily physiotherapy is required to deal with it.

Pinpointing the CF gene led to the isolation of a membrane protein that malfunctions in the disease. This is the **CFTR** – short for **cystic fibrosis transmembrane regulator** – protein. Scientists think that this protein probably acts as a gated channel that lets chloride ions through. In CF there are faults in the primary sequence of the protein in the gate region. Somehow the faulty sequence stops this molecular gate from opening, effectively blocking the chloride ion channel. Comparison of the sequence of CFTR with that of other sequences by scanning a protein database suggests that it may be an ATP-dependent pump involved in active transport rather than a passive ion channel.

Further research should lead to ways of unlocking the molecular gate in the CFTR, giving new hope to thousands of CF sufferers.

QUESTION    **6 How does knowing which protein is involved in CF improve the prospects for treatment?**

## Summary of Chapter 4

1 Lipids are a chemically diverse group of biologically active compounds that share the characteristic of being insoluble in water. Lipids include fats and oils, which are based on fatty acids and can be utilised as a concentrated source of energy and as protection and insulation on the surface of organisms.

2 Another lipid, cholesterol, is a steroid that is the source of hormones and other important molecules in the cell. Cholesterol can cause atherosclerosis when high levels of it circulate in the blood.

3 Phospholipids are molecules with a polar and a non-polar end. They are a major component of cell membranes, where they form a bilayer. Membranes also contain protein and carbohydrate.

4   The fluid mosaic model describes how phospholipids move laterally within the bilayer, constrained by the presence of cholesterol molecules embedded in the layer at intervals. Cell membranes separate the cell from its environment and are selectively permeable, allowing materials into and out of the cell. Proteins embedded in the membrane allow both diffusion and active transport. Some of these are attached to carbohydrate groups on the outer surface of the membrane.

## Examination questions

1   (a) What do you understand by the term lipid?
    (b) Describe the roles of lipids in cell structure.
    (c) Describe the importance of lipids in
        (i) steroid hormone actions in animals
        (ii) waterproofing in animals. (O & C)

2   (a) (i) What is meant by an essential fatty acid?
        (ii) Name three chemical elements present in fatty acids.
    (b) State two ways in which a phospholipid differs from a triglyceride.
    (c) Explain how the structure of phospholipids is related to their function in cell membranes. (London)

3   Figure 4.7 shows a model of the plasma membrane (cell surface membrane).
    (a) State two functions of proteins in the plasma membrane.
    (b) Explain the importance of phospholipids in the structure of the plasma membrane.
    (c) (i) Suggest one function of the part labelled X.
        (ii) Copy the diagram and write the word OUTSIDE on the surface of the membrane which faces outward. State the reason for your choice. (London)

4   (a) Outline the basic molecular structure of membranes.
    (b) Describe the different methods by which substances move across cell membranes. (UCLES)

**Figure 4.7**

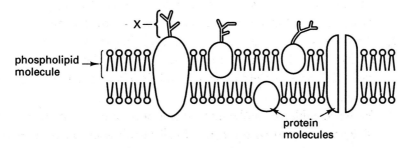

phospholipid molecule →

protein molecules

# chapter 5

# Carbohydrates

As the name suggests, carbohydrates contain carbon and the elements of water – hydrogen and oxygen. Carbohydrates range from small molecules such as glucose, $C_6H_{12}O_6$, to polymers such as cellulose. Carbohydrates are found in all cells. Sometimes they are part of larger molecules. For example, ribose is part of the RNA molecule, while many eukaryotic proteins called **glycoproteins** have a carbohydrate 'label' attached to them.

Carbohydrates are the main energy source of the cell. They are also important building materials, particularly for plant cells. In the early 1980s a new role for carbohydrates was discovered: they help proteins to communicate with each other by acting as an identity tag on glycoproteins.

## 5.1    Carbohydrates come in a range of sizes

Carbohydrates occur either as fairly small molecules (**monosaccharides** and **disaccharides**) or as polymers (**polysaccharides**) (Figure 5.1).

Monosaccharides are sometimes known as **sugars**. They contain between three and ten carbon atoms per molecule. The most important ones in the cell are **trioses** (three carbons), **pentoses** (five carbons) and **hexoses** (six carbons). The presence of hydroxyl groups means that monosaccharides form extensive hydrogen bonds with water, making them very soluble. This solubility means that they are readily available to be broken down, to release energy in the form of ATP.

When two monosaccharides condense, an oxygen bridge known as a **glycosidic bond** forms. The structures of some common disaccharides (often also called **sugars**) are shown in Figure 5.1. Condensation of many monosaccharides leads to insoluble polymeric molecules such as **starch** and **cellulose**. The occurrence of some common carbohydrates is shown in Table 5.1.

## 5.2    Starch is the source of texture and sweetness in many foods

Starch is a mixture of two polymers – **amylose** and **amylopectin**. Both are made up of glucose units, but amylose is a straight-chain molecule while amylopectin is branched. The way in which the glycosidic bonds in amylose are arranged

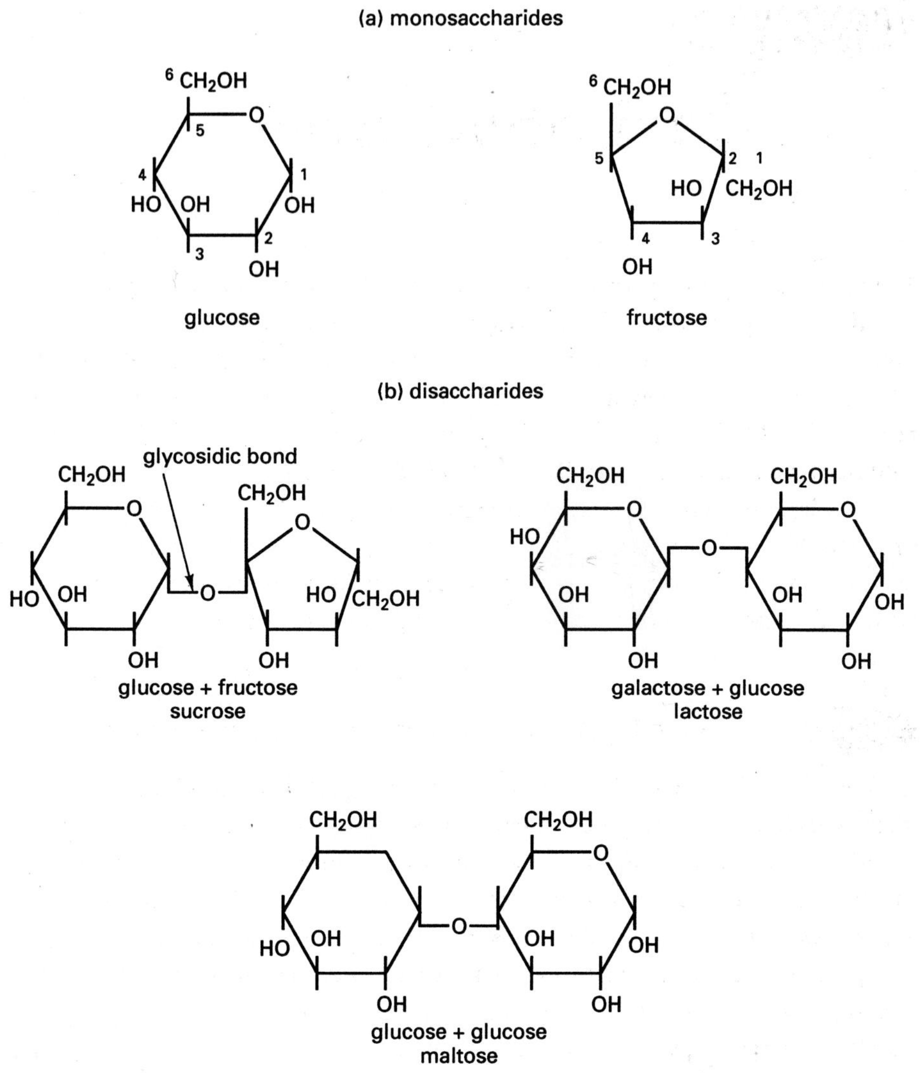
(a) monosaccharides
6 CH2OH
O
5
4
1
HO OH
OH
3
2
OH
glucose
6 CH2OH
O
5
2 1
HO CH2OH
4
3
OH
fructose
(b) disaccharides
glycosidic bond
CH2OH
CH2OH
O
O
HO OH
O
HO CH2OH
OH
OH
glucose + fructose
sucrose
CH2OH
CH2OH
O
HO
O
O
OH
OH
OH
OH
OH
galactose + glucose
lactose
CH2OH
CH2OH
O
HO OH
O
OH
OH
OH
OH
glucose + glucose
maltose

**Figure 5.1** Some important sugars (carbon and hydrogen atoms in the rings are not shown).

makes it easy for the molecule to form a helix, held together by hydrogen bonds (in Figure 5.2, compare the structures of amylose and cellulose). The helices pack together in starch granules, which are a major component of flour and potatoes.

When starch granules are heated in water, the hydrogen bonds in the starch helices break down. At the same time, water molecules rush into the granules and hydrogen bond all over the starch molecules. This sudden swelling of the starch molecules causes the thickening of sauces, such as gravy and custard, on cooking. Once they are released from their granules, the starch molecules tangle with each other, leading to a further increase in the viscosity of the mixture.

**Table 5.1   The range of carbohydrates in living organisms**

| Carbohydrate(s) | Where found |
| --- | --- |
| *Monosaccharides* | |
| Ribose | component of RNA |
| Deoxyribose | component of DNA |
| Glucose | nectar, blood, leaves; the main fuel of cells |
| Fructose | honey, fruit |
| Xylose | plants, as 'wood sugar' |
| *Disaccharides* | |
| Sucrose | sugar beet, sugar cane |
| Lactose | milk |
| Maltose | germinating seeds, alimentary canal – from breakdown of starch |
| *Polysaccharides* | |
| Cellulose | all plant cells; most abundant polymer on Earth |
| Chitin (also contains nitrogen) | insect wings and crustacean shells; second most abundant polymer on Earth |
| Starch | leaves and tubers – plant energy storage compound |
| Glycogen | muscle and liver – animal energy storage compound |

Glucose units can be snipped off the branched chains of amylopectin by the enzyme **amylase**, which hydrolyses the glycosidic bond. This reaction is used to refuel plant cells from their starch stores whenever glucose is in short supply. These plant amylases start to work on starch in flour when bread dough is kneaded, producing a mixture of sugar, maltose and short-chain polysaccharides known as **dextrins**. These sugars are fermented by yeast to produce the carbon dioxide that makes the bread rise on baking, giving the loaf its springy texture. Also produced by fermentation are alcohols, which contribute to the aroma and taste of freshly baked bread.

While the bread is being baked, the remaining sugars decompose to give steam and a complex dark mixture called caramel, which gives the crust its characteristic brown colour and also plays a part in the flavour of the bread.

QUESTION   **1 Describe the chemistry of toast making.**

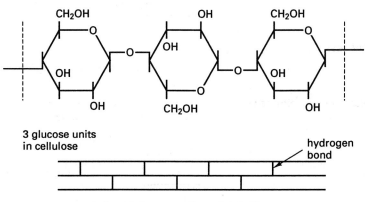

Figure 5.2

Polysaccharide

structures.

(a) the structure of starch

CH₂OH    CH₂OH    CH₂OH

3 glucose units in amylose

hydrogen bond   chains of glucose units pack into a helix

(b) the structure of cellulose

CH₂OH    OH    CH₂OH

3 glucose units in cellulose

hydrogen bond

chains of glucose units pack into fibres

## Sweeteners

If you chew bread, it soon begins to taste sweet. This is because amylase in saliva starts to break down the starch into a mixture of dextrins and glucose, which tastes sweet. The industrial equivalents of partly digested bread are starch syrup (long-chain dextrins), glucose syrup (short-chain dextrins) and glucose, all produced by the action of fungal amylase on corn starch (Figure 5.3).

Starch syrup is not particularly sweet, but is used as a thickener to give a smooth texture in products such as frozen mousses. Glucose syrup is used as a 'background' sweetener in biscuits, cakes and toffees. It is less sweet than sucrose.

Glucose produced by this process can be turned into high-fructose syrup (HFS). Glucose and fructose are closely related chemically – they have the same formula and they are both monosaccharides. The difference is that their atoms are arranged differently (Figure 5.1). Glucose and fructose are **isomers**.

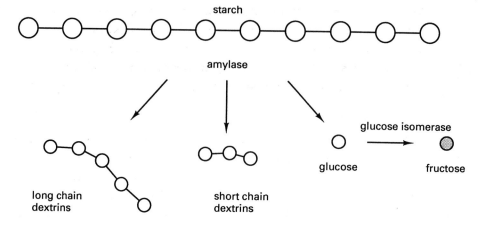

Figure 5.3 The products of the enzymatic breakdown of starch.

In the production of HFS, the enzyme **glucose isomerase** is used to turn the glucose into fructose. HFS is actually a mixture of glucose and fructose. More than 3 million tonnes of HFS is produced annually, mainly in countries without local sources of sucrose.

Fructose is one-and-a-half times sweeter than ordinary sugar (sucrose), but like all sugars it is a fuel. Excess input of any chemical fuel causes humans and other animals to put on weight. But sweetness seems to increase the palatability of food. The desire for the sweet sensation without weight gain has led to the development of non-carbohydrate sweeteners (Table 5.2).

**Table 5.2   Sweetness of some substances compared to sucrose**

| Sweetener | Sweetness | Use |
| --- | --- | --- |
| *Carbohydrates* | | |
| Sucrose | 1.0 | ordinary sugar |
| Glucose | 0.7 | background sweetener |
| Fructose | 1.5 | diabetic sugar substitute |
| Sucralose | 500 | under development – low-calorie cakes, etc. |
| *Peptides and proteins* | | |
| Aspartame | 200 | used widely in the UK |
| Thaumatin | 3000 | chewing gum and animal feed |
| *Other* | | |
| Saccharin | 300 | used similarly to aspartame in UK |
| Cyclamate | 30 | food and drink, but banned in UK as a cancer risk |

**2** Sucralose will be the first 'low-calorie' sweetener to be used in cakes and biscuits. The body does not recognise it as a fuel and will not metabolise it in the same way as it would sugar. Suppose you bake a slimmer's cake with sucralose and adapt your recipe, which calls for 100 g of sugar. How much sucralose would you need?

QUESTION

## Fat substitutes

Dietary intake of saturated fats is linked to heart disease, obesity and the development of specific cancers. Fats provide a pleasant mouthfeel and taste to food, making it hard to cut down to the limits of around 97 g (men) or 74 g (women) as recommended by the Government in 1990. New products make use of the structure of carbohydrates to provide a backbone on which to attach fatty acids in place of glycerol. These products are fat substitutes. When six or more fatty acids are attached to the carbohydrate backbone, the fat substitute cannot be broken down by lipase enzymes, so it is not digested or absorbed by the body. These fat substitutes retain the mouthfeel and cooking character-istics of fat, owing to the presence of fatty acids, but they do not contribute to calorie intake and bypass the health problems associated with normal fat intakes. For example, olestra is a mixture of sucrose esters with various fatty acids (so the sucrose is acting like the glycerol backbone in triglycerides). Because of its stability at high temperatures, olestra's main use will be in situations where food is prepared at high temperatures such as frying and baking. This means that, so far, it is the only fat substitute which could be used to make fast foods such as fish and chips a healthier option.

### 5.3    Carbohydrates help to build cell walls and insect wings

Cellulose is the most abundant carbon compound on Earth. It is a polymer in which glucose units are linked through oxygen bridges in such a way that each glucose molecule is inverted, relative to its neighbours, as shown in Figure 5.2. This 'head-to-tail' linkage allows the formation of long chains, which can connect together sideways, through hydrogen bonds, to form strong yet flexible fibres.

Cellulose is the main component of plant cell walls; it is also found in the cell walls of some fungi. In wood, cellulose is embedded in a framework of **lignocellulose**. Lignocellulose is a mixture of two polymers – **lignin**, which gives wood its dark colour, and a polysaccharide known as **hemicellulose**. This inner structure accounts for the toughness of wood.

A total of $10^{15}$ kg of cellulose is synthesised and broken down each year, world-wide. It is built up in plants from photosynthesis. It is completely insoluble, and is not broken down by plant enzymes. However, some bacteria can use cellulose as a source of food and energy because they contain enzymes known as **cellulases** that can decompose the large cellulose molecule into simpler molecules. Such bacteria colonise the guts of herbivores such as sheep and cows – an arrangement that benefits both organisms, as the animals can use the products of cellulose digestion. Similarly termites, or white ants, are able to live on wood because their guts contain protozoa that produce cellulase.

Humans cannot digest cellulose, which is the main component of dietary fibre. It adds bulk to food, enhancing its movement through the intestine. Although it has no nutritional value, it is an important part of the diet. Populations eating a diet high in fibre tend to have lower rates of diseases such as bowel cancer.

The fibrous nature of cellulose has been exploited in the development of the textile and paper industries (see Table 5.3).

**Table 5.3 Some uses of cellulose**

| Plant source | Use |
| --- | --- |
| Cotton | textiles – almost pure cellulose, very strong |
| Flax | linen textiles |
| Rattan | cane furniture |
| Coconut | coir fibre surrounding shell, used for mattresses, ropes and brushes |
| Sisal | ropes |
| Willow | baskets |
| Wood pulp | paper, viscose textiles when treated with alkali and acid – five trees could clothe one person for a lifetime |

QUESTION **3 The most recent addition to 'biological' detergents, which contain enzymes, has been cellulase. It conditions cotton-based fabrics whose surfaces have become roughened by handling and washing. How do these new detergents work?**

**Chitin**, the main component of insect wings and the exoskeletons of scorpions and crabs, is the second most abundant polymer on Earth. In its structure it resembles cellulose, but it has a group of atoms called an N-acetyl group in place of one of the hydroxyl groups. This group contains nitrogen and oxygen atoms, both of which can take part in hydrogen bonding. This means that chitin can form more hydrogen bonds between neighbouring polysaccharide chains than cellulose can – therefore it is a tougher material.

QUESTION **4 Design and carry out an experiment to test the strength of cellulose and compare it to some other commonly used structural materials. How can you account for the strength of cellulose in molecular terms?**

### 5.4    Carbohydrates attached to proteins and lipids play important roles in the cell

Carbohydrates are often attached to eukaryotic proteins as one of the final steps in their synthesis. These proteins are known as **glycoproteins**. Carbohydrates can also be linked to lipids to form **glycolipids**.

Within the last ten years it has been realised that the carbohydrates on these molecules have an important function. Because carbohydrates are so water-soluble, they can orient proteins and lipids within the cell membrane – they always point outwards on the cell membrane, where the water is. They can also help proteins to recognise each other within and between cells by adding a distinctive molecular feature to the protein surface.

In rheumatoid arthritis, proteins lack one vital sugar on their polysaccharide tag. This can be used as a basis for a diagnostic test and, eventually, perhaps as a therapy for the disease. The parasites that cause sleeping sickness and related diseases often alter the carbohydrates on their outer protein coat, fooling the body's defences. Finally, carbohydrates on the outer protein coat of the HIV virus, which causes AIDS, play a part in its attack on the human immune system.

### 5.5    Carbohydrates can be distinguished by chemical tests

The common monosaccharides such as glucose and fructose are **reducing sugars**. Although they exist in the cell mainly in the ring forms shown in Figure 5.1, they can also exist in the straight-chain forms shown in Figure 5.4. These forms show clearly that glucose is an example of an **aldose** sugar, containing an aldehyde group. Fructose, its isomer, has a ketone group and is known as a **ketose** sugar.

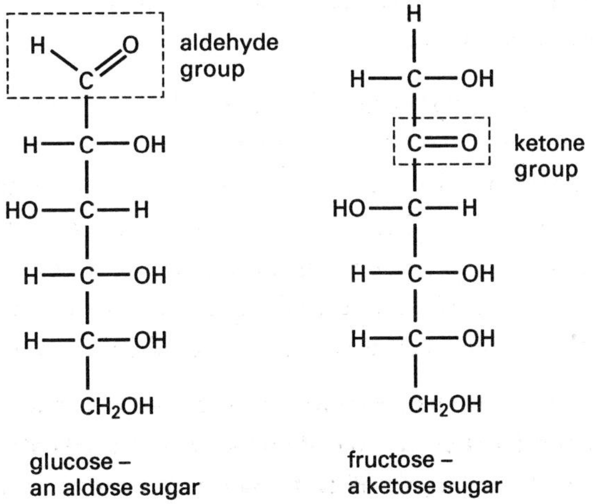

**Figure 5.4** Straight-chain forms of glucose and fructose.

glucose –
an aldose sugar

fructose –
a ketose sugar

Both aldoses and ketoses have reducing properties. This is the basis for tests with Benedict's or Fehling's solutions, which are used, alongside other tests, for distinguishing between different carbohydrates. These tests are summarised in Table 5.4.

**Table 5.4   Chemical tests for carbohydrates. Use 1–2 per cent solutions or suspensions of carbohydrates in these tests**

| Test | Observation | Conclusion |
| --- | --- | --- |
| *Benedict's test* | | |
| Add 2 cm³ Benedict's solution to an equal volume of carbohydrate solution; boil gently for a few minutes | green-yellow colour; may be brick-red precipitate | monosaccharide present (e.g. fructose, glucose), some disaccharides (e.g. maltose) |
| *Fehling's test* | | |
| Add 1 cm³ Fehling's solution A and Fehling's solution B to 2 cm³ carbohydrate solution; boil gently for a few minutes | as for Benedict's test above | as for Benedict's test above |
| *Iodine/potassium iodide* | | |
| Add a few drops of iodine dissolved in potassium iodide solution to carbohydrate solution | blue-black colour | starch is present |

Carbohydrates that give a positive result in the tests are called reducing sugars. The most common **non-reducing sugar** is sucrose. This gives a positive result with Benedict's and Fehling's solutions if a 2 cm³ sample is first boiled with a 1 cm³ dilute hydrochloric acid for one minute, cooled and then neutralised with solid sodium hydrogencarbonate (check for neutrality with pH paper). Then carry out either of the first two tests in the table.

QUESTION   **5 How would you follow the progress of the reaction of starch with amylase?**

## Summary of Chapter 5

1   Carbohydrates contain carbon, hydrogen and oxygen. They occur either as small molecules or as polymers.

2   Starch and cellulose are both polysaccharides, which differ in their properties because of the way in which their basic glucose units are linked.

3   Starch is the energy store of plants. It can be broken down by amylase into dextrins and glucose.

4 Cellulose is a structural polymer that occurs in all plants. It has many uses including paper and textile manufacture. It is broken down to glucose by cellulase enzymes.

5 Glucose and fructose are reducing sugars. Reducing sugars can be identified by their ability to produce a red precipitate of copper(i) from a solution containing the copper(ii) ion. Starch gives a blue colour with iodine, which binds inside its helical structure.

## Examination questions

1 (a) Name three biologically important disaccharides and state where they can be found.
   (b) Starch and cellulose are high molecular weight polysaccharides. Which hexose sugar forms their basic unit?
   (c) What is the essential structural difference between starch and cellulose?
   (d) Starch is an important storage compound. In what structure is it characteristically located in plant cells?
   (e) Name the storage polysaccharide found in mammals.
   (f) Name the organ where it occurs in large amounts.
   (g) Where is it deposited in the cell? (WJEC)

2 Write an essay on the importance in living organisms of the size and shape of organic molecules. (London)

3 Describe with practical details how you would compare the reducing sugar content of two different varieties of grape. (London)

4 (a) Copy and complete Table 5.5 giving the general formula, one named example and one function in living organisms of each of the carbohydrates listed.

**Table 5.5**

| Carbohydrate | General formula | Example | Function in living organisms |
| --- | --- | --- | --- |
| Pentose | | | |
| Disaccharide | | | |

   (b) Suggest why the main storage compounds of animals are usually lipids, whereas those of plants are usually carbohydrates. (London)

# chapter 6

# Photosynthesis and respiration

Life on Earth depends upon **photosynthesis**, which traps the light energy of the Sun and converts it into the chemical energy that is stored in carbohydrates. Living things then extract this chemical energy to power their cells by the process of **respiration**. Although there are some variations on this theme – bacteria that obtain energy from metal ions rather than from carbon-based fuels, for example – the linked processes of photosynthesis and respiration are of primary importance for most living organisms.

## 6.1 Plants make carbohydrates by photosynthesis

The overall equation of photosynthesis is given by:

$$6CO_2 + 6H_2O \rightarrow C_6H_{12}O_6 + 6O_2$$

glucose

Photosynthesis requires a source of light energy (usually the Sun) and a pigment that can absorb this light – usually chlorophyll, although other pigments are used in some bacteria.

Photosynthesis is not as simple as this equation suggests; it consists of a set of reactions, all of which are controlled by enzymes. Looking at the factors that affect the rate of photosynthesis gives some understanding of the nature of these reactions.

The rate of photosynthesis can be found by measuring the volume of oxygen that is evolved in a given time. The factors that affect this rate are light intensity, carbon dioxide concentration and temperature. When light intensity is varied, for example, the graph of Figure 6.1 is obtained. Initially, rate increases with intensity. In other words, light is the **limiting factor** in this region of the graph. However, the rate then reaches a plateau at a certain limiting value of light intensity.

This is strong evidence that photosynthesis is a two-stage process. The first stage is the **light reaction**. The second stage is called the **dark reaction**. Increasing light intensity affects the first stage, but not the second. This is

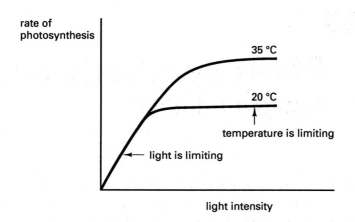

rate of
photosynthesis

35 °C

20 °C

temperature is limiting

light is limiting

light intensity

Figure 6.1 The
effect of light
intensity on the
rate of
photosynthesis.

confirmed by altering a factor that affects mainly the second stage – temperature. This causes the plateau to shift upwards. At constant light intensity, the higher the temperature, the higher the rate of photosynthesis, with a maximum occurring at around 35 °C. At higher temperatures the enzymes involved begin to lose their activity.

Referring back to the equation of photosynthesis, the water is split up into hydrogen and oxygen in the light reaction, using the energy of sunlight, while the carbon dioxide is transformed into glucose in the dark reaction.

**QUESTION**

1  **Using Figure 6.1 as a guide, sketch and label a graph showing the dependence of the rate of photosynthesis on carbon dioxide concentration. Comment on its shape.**

## 6.2    The chloroplast

The chloroplast is the site of photosynthesis in green plants. The internal structure of the chloroplast is well adapted for the chemistry of photosynthesis, as shown in Figure 6.2. A pair of membranes encloses the fluid-filled **stroma**. Inside the stroma are disc-shaped cavities called **thylakoids**, which are stacked in piles called **grana** (singular **granum**). Grana are linked together by membranes called **lamellae**.

The thylakoid membrane contains pigments – chemicals that can absorb light. The most important for photosynthesis is **chlorophyll a**, whose chemical structure is shown in Figure 6.3. It is chemically related to haem, the iron-containing pigment of the haemoglobin found in red blood cells, but contains magnesium (Mg) instead of iron (Fe). Chlorophyll *a* appears green because it absorbs the red and blue wavelengths of white light and reflects the green wavelengths. This can be confirmed by examining the **absorption spectrum** of chlorophyll (Figure 6.4, see p.82).

Figure 6.2 (a)
Electron
micrograph of
a chloroplast
(magnification
about 10 000).
(b) Chloroplast
structure.

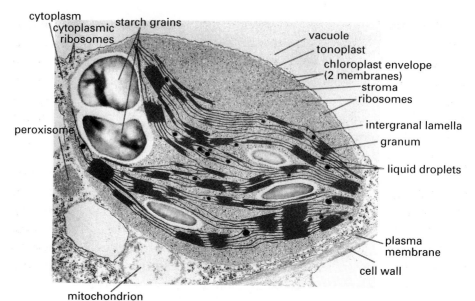

(a)

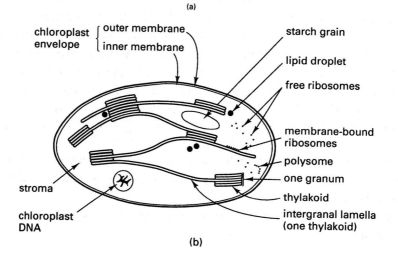

(b)

Figure 6.3
Structure of
chlorophylls.

$C_{20}H_{39}$ phytol
tail (hydrocarbon)

flat, square porphyrin
head with magnesium
at centre

Key
X –$CH_3$ in chlorophyll *a*
  –CHO in chlorophyll *b*

To obtain the absorption spectrum of chlorophyll, a beam of white light is shone through a chlorophyll solution. The light emerging from this solution is passed through a prism, which splits it up into different wavelengths. The intensities of light at each different wavelength are measured by a spectrophotometer and the results displayed as in Figure 6.4. The high absorption displayed in the red and blue ends of the spectrum suggest that these are the wavelengths that the chlorophyll molecule has absorbed from the white light as it passed through the solution.

This absorption of light at these wavelengths by chlorophyll *a* is the first step in the light reaction. If the rate of photosynthesis is measured at different wavelengths, a graph known as the **action spectrum** is obtained (Figure 6.4). The action spectrum is important because it shows that chlorophyll *a* is the main pigment involved in photosynthesis. **Carotenoids** and **xanthophylls** protect chlorophyll from excess light by absorbing it, and also react with some of the oxygen produced, preventing it from damaging the cell.

The structure of the chlorophyll molecule allows its electrons to wander freely over the cyclic portion (the 'head') with the magnesium ion at the centre. Light carries its energy in units or 'packets' known as **photons**. The amount of energy carried by a photon depends upon the wavelength of the light – blue light photons carry more energy than red light photons. When photons interact with chlorophyll molecules, energy is transferred from the photon to the molecule. This allows the excitation of an electron in the chlorophyll molecule and its transfer to other molecules in the photosynthetic system.

**2** **What feature of the chlorophyll molecule allows it to embed itself in the thylakoid membrane? Sketch a diagram to show the orientation of the chlorophyll molecule in the membrane.**    QUESTION

**3** **From its absorption spectrum, what colour would you expect a carotenoid to be?**

### 6.3   The light reaction of photosynthesis

The light reaction provides the two essential ingredients for the dark reaction – **ATP** and **NADPH**. Building up glucose from carbon dioxide requires energy, so the dark reactions are driven by ATP. In glucose, carbon is more highly reduced than it is in carbon dioxide, so a reducing agent, NADPH, is also required.

**Figure 6.4 The spectrum of chlorophyll. (a) The experimental set-up.**

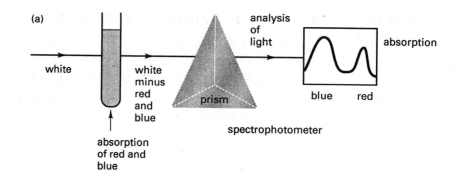

**(b) Dispersion of light by a prism.**

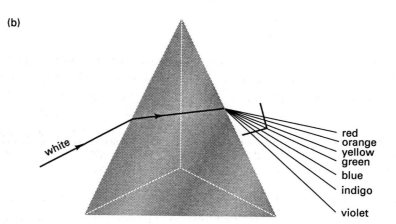

**(c) The action spectrum of photosynthesis compared to the absorption spectrum for the pigment molecules present.**

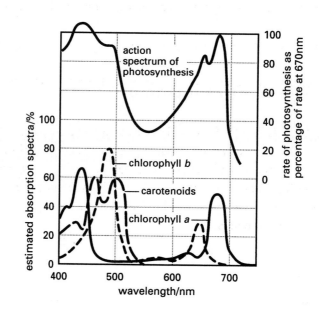

# Hydrogen carriers in biochemical reactions

Wherever oxidation and reduction reactions take place in the cell, molecules known as **hydrogen carriers** are involved. They accept hydrogen atoms from molecules known as hydrogen **donors**, and donate them to other molecules known as hydrogen **acceptors**. In other words, they act as a bridge between the hydrogen donor and the hydrogen acceptor as follows:

$$AH_2 \quad + \quad X \quad \rightarrow \quad XH_2 \quad + \quad A$$

hydrogen    hydrogen
donor      carrier

$$B \quad + \quad XH_2 \quad \rightarrow \quad X \quad + \quad BH_2$$

hydrogen
acceptor

There are three of these hydrogen carriers – **nicotinamide adenine dinucleotide** (NAD), **nicotinamide adenine dinucleotide phosphate** (NADP) and **flavin adenine dinucleotide** (FAD). Their structures are shown in Figure 6.5. Note that, like the nucleic acids, these are nucleotides. The groups linked to the nucleotides are derived from the B vitamins. NAD and NADP are **coenzymes**, while FAD is a **prosthetic group**. They carry hydrogen atoms in oxidation–reduction (redox) reactions as shown in Figure 6.5:

1. In aqueous solution NAD and NADP are positively charged, as shown. They accept a pair of hydrogen atoms from a hydrogen donor. If the hydrogen atoms are considered as a pair of protons and a pair of electrons, then the products are reduced coenzymes NADH and NADPH, together with an associated proton.
2. The reduced coenzymes transfer their two hydrogen atoms to a hydrogen acceptor.
3. FAD is neutral in solution. It accepts a pair of hydrogen atoms to become reduced FAD (i.e. $FADH_2$).
4. Reduced FAD gives up its pair of hydrogen atoms to a hydrogen acceptor.

Whether NAD, NADP or FAD is used as a hydrogen carrier depends upon the exact nature of the oxidation–reduction reaction. These reactions are a key feature of photosynthesis and respiration, so the hydrogen carriers play a major role in both processes. Of course, all reactions are under the control of enzymes – the class of enzymes involved in the reactions just described is known as the **dehydrogenases**.

Figure 6.5 The
structures and
reactions of
hydrogen
carriers.

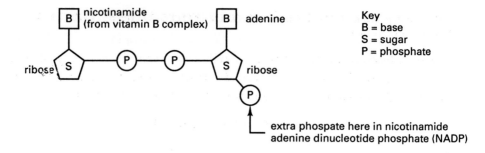

Key
B = base
S = sugar
P = phosphate

extra phospate here in nicotinamide
adenine dinucleotide phosphate (NADP)

(a) nicotinamide adenine dinucleotide (NAD) and NADP

riboflavin
(vitamin
B₂)

ribitol
(an alcohol)

(b) flavin adenine dinucleotide (FAD)

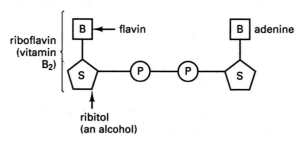

from hydrogen donor
↓
(1) NAD(P)⁺ + 2H⁺ + 2e⁻ → NAD(P)H + H⁺
coenzymes        2H         reduced coenzymes

(2) NAD(P)H + H⁺ → NAD(P)⁺ + 2H
↓
to hydrogen acceptor

from hydrogen donor
↓
(3) FAD + 2H → FADH₂
reduced FAD

(4) FADH₂ → FAD + 2H
↓
to hydrogen acceptor

## The oxygen evolved in photosynthesis comes from water

This can be demonstrated by radio-labelling the water. A heavy oxygen atom, $^{18}O$, is used for this purpose. The radio-labelled atom is shown as $O^*$. The results of the experiment are shown in the following equation:

$$6CO_2 + 6H_2O^* \rightarrow C_6H_{12}O_6 + 6O_2^*$$

The heavy oxygen produced was detected by a mass spectrometer, an instrument that distinguishes between different atoms on the basis of their mass.

This led to the idea that the main chemical reaction in the light stage is:

$$H_2O \rightarrow 2H^+ + 2e^- + \tfrac{1}{2}O_2$$

This is called the **photolysis** of water, because it uses the energy of light to split one of the chemical bonds in the water molecule.

**4 Describe a further experiment that you could do to confirm that the oxygen given off in photosynthesis comes from water.**    QUESTION

## The Hill reaction shows that chloroplasts can reduce electron acceptors

In 1939, Robert Hill of Cambridge University showed that isolated chloroplasts could produce oxygen from water, when illuminated, and that various oxidising reagents were reduced at the same time. For example, the blue dye DCPIP can be added to the reaction mixture as a marker. When it is reduced, it loses its colour.

This suggests that electrons produced by light absorption in photosynthesis can eventually be accepted by electron acceptors such as NADP in the following reaction:

$$NADP^+ + 2H^+ + 2e^- \rightarrow NADP + H^+$$

The electrons are shuttled along a chain of molecules embedded in the thylakoid membrane before they are eventually accepted by NADP. These molecules are electron carriers; they are either proteins or smaller molecules that are capable of ready oxidation and reduction. They accept the electrons and then hand them on to the next electron carrier in the chain.

**5 Is NADP an oxidising or a reducing agent?**    QUESTION

## A pH gradient drives the production of ATP

In 1966, Andre Jagendorf showed that chloroplasts can synthesise ATP in the dark if there is a pH gradient across the thylakoid membrane. First he soaked intact chloroplasts in a buffer of pH 4 for several hours (see Figure 6.6) to equalise the pH inside and outside the membrane. Then he suddenly changed the buffer to one of pH 8, adding the ingredients for ATP synthesis at the same time. Now there is a pH gradient across the thylakoid membrane. There is a higher concentration of protons inside (low pH) the membrane than outside (high pH). So protons flow from the inside to the outside of the membrane. As they do so, ATP is synthesised. (This idea will be developed further in the last section of this chapter.)

During photosynthesis, this pH gradient occurs naturally. As electrons flow along the chain of electron acceptors in the thylakoid membrane, energy is released, which allows protons to be pumped across the membrane and to build up inside the thylakoid space.

**Figure 6.6 ATP synthesis is linked to a pH gradient.**

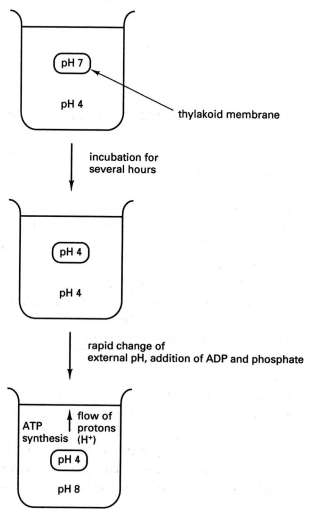

QUESTION

**6 Why did Jagendorf's experiment work in the dark?**

The production of ATP through this mechanism is called **photophos-phorylation**. The energy of sunlight has been converted to chemical potential energy, stored in the proton gradient. This is then converted into the chemical energy of ATP. The main features of the light reaction are summarised in Figure 6.7.

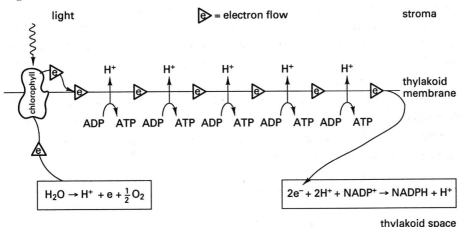

Figure 6.7 Summary of the light reactions of photosynthesis.

## Photosynthesis is a model for alternative energy sources

The flow of protons across the membrane in photosynthesis is not just a pH gradient. As the protons are charged, it is also an electric potential difference. For many years, scientists have been trying to exploit this proton pumping as a source of electrical power.

One of the first projects was based on *Halobacterium halobium*, a photosynthetic bacterium that thrives in the salty waters of the Dead Sea. Its membranes are covered with purple patches, which contain the pigment bacteriorhodopsin. When the Sun shines on the purple patches, protons are driven across the membrane to the interior of the cell. The purple patches can generate electrical currents in the laboratory and they work even when the cells themselves have been destroyed. The process is very inefficient – only about 1 per cent of the solar energy, at best, can be turned into electricity. But scientists in Israel working on the purple patches say that they could be useful in hot countries as a source of domestic power.

Meanwhile, chemists in the United States have been working on molecular 'funnels' – synthetic molecules with structures based on that of chlorophyll. The 'funnels' are designed to improve on Nature by trapping more sunlight than chlorophyll does and generating more electrical charge. These molecules can convert up to 67 per cent of the solar energy into electricity, comparing favourably with silicon-based solar cells, whose efficiency is about 20 per cent.

QUESTIONS

7 How would you grow large amounts of *Halobacterium halobium* for a purple patch project? (Hint: consider the conditions under which these microbes would thrive and design a fermenter system that incorporates them.)

8 How would you attempt to separate out the membranes and make a working solar cell with them? (Hint: you will have to isolate the membrane from the rest of the bacterial cell.)

9 Which part of the chlorophyll molecule should be retained in the design of a molecular 'funnel'?

10 What are the advantages and disadvantages of photosynthetic batteries?

### 6.4    The dark reaction of photosynthesis

Our understanding of the dark reaction of photosynthesis is due to the work of Melvin Calvin and his team in the 1940s. Calvin grew *Chlorella*, an alga, in the presence of radio-labelled carbon dioxide. He illuminated the cells, allowed them to photosynthesise for a short time and then killed them by dropping them into hot methanol.

He then used chromatography to find out which of the compounds that the plant had synthesised contained a $^{14}C$ label. Although the radioactive compounds are invisible, they show up as black spots on photographic film placed over the chromatogram.

The first thing Calvin discovered was that photosynthesis is a very rapid process. After only 60 seconds, his chromatogram was covered with radioactive spots, showing that the radio-labelled carbon dioxide had already been built up into many sugars and amino acids (Figure 6.8a). Reducing the time of the experiment to 5 seconds captured the first stages of photosynthesis, however (Figure 6.8b). Calvin identified **glyceraldehyde-3-phosphate** (G3P) as a key intermediate in the dark reaction. From this, he went on to work out how G3P is formed and is then used to build up more complex compounds.

**Figure 6.8
Chromatograms
of *Chlorella*
extract after
incubation with
radio-labelled
$CO_2$.
From:
Biochemistry
2/e by Lubert
Stryer.
Copyright ©
1981 by Lubert
Stryer.
Reprinted with
permission of
W.H. Freeman
and Company.**

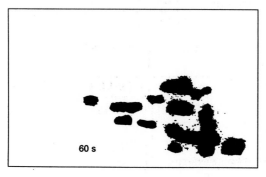

60 s

(a)

3-Phosphoglycerate
(G3P)

5 s

(b)

First, carbon dioxide reacts with a pentose sugar called **ribulose bisphosphate** (RBP), which has two phosphate groups. This reaction is catalysed by the enzyme **ribulose bisphosphate carboxylase** (**Rubisco**), said to be the most abundant protein on Earth. An unstable hexose is formed, which is rapidly broken down into two molecules of G3P. Some of this G3P is recycled to form more RBP. This part of the photosynthetic process is known as the **Calvin cycle**.

G3P also acts as a metabolic 'pool', which can be drawn on for the synthesis of many other products, as shown in Figure 6.9. The first sugar made is a triose. To synthesise this from G3P, a reduction is necessary, and an energy input. Here the ATP and the NADPH synthesised in the light reactions are used. NADPH reduces G3P to form the triose. Glucose, and other sugars, can then be synthesised from the triose. Excess glucose is stored as starch. G3P is also the source of fats and proteins in the plant.

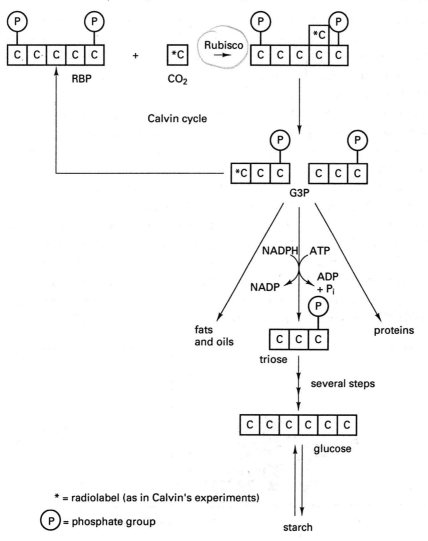

Figure 6.9 The dark reactions of photosynthesis. The carbon backbone is shown as blocks for simplicity, and many of the molecular details are omitted.

QUESTION    **11 How have radio-labelling experiments helped us to understand the chemistry of photosynthesis?**

The process described above is not the only method of photosynthesis, but it is the most common one in plants that grow in temperate regions. Because the main metabolic intermediate has three carbon atoms, it is known as **$C_3$ photosynthesis**.

## $C_3$ and $C_4$ photosynthesis

Plants in tropical regions, such as sugar cane, need to conserve water, so they keep the stomata in their leaves closed for much of the time, leading to low carbon dioxide levels in their cells. A different mode of fixing carbon dioxide, called **$C_4$ photosynthesis**, has evolved in these plants. Carbon dioxide reacts with a three-carbon compound called **phosphoenolpyruvate** (PEP) instead of with RBP. This leads to a metabolic intermediate known as **oxaloacetic acid** that has four carbon atoms in place of G3P. The $C_4$ pathway operates efficiently at lower carbon dioxide levels. Under similar conditions, $C_4$ plants make more glucose per unit leaf area than do $C_3$ plants.

Of the world's major food plants, only maize, sorghum, sugar cane and millet carry out $C_4$ photosynthesis. Wheat, rice, barley, potato and soybean are $C_3$ plants. A major concern that arises from the prospect of global warming is how increased temperatures and carbon dioxide levels will affect world agriculture. While increased carbon dioxide will stimulate photosynthesis in both types, the effect is likely to be greater for $C_3$ plants, while the $C_4$ plants will probably adapt better to the higher temperatures. It is difficult to make firm predictions, but $C_3$ plants may do better overall. While this has the obvious advantage of allowing $C_3$ crops to extend their range, it may also mean that $C_3$ weeds will prosper at the expense of $C_4$ crops.

## 6.5    Respiration fuels all living cells

Glucose is the main fuel of living organisms. The stepwise, enzyme-controlled dismantling of the glucose molecule to extract energy from it is known as **respiration**. Respiration is therefore a process undergone by all cells. The overall equation of respiration is:

$$C_6H_{12}O_6 + 6O_2 \rightarrow 6CO_2 + 6H_2O$$

**glucose**

However, the most important product of respiration, ATP, does not actually appear in the above equation. Each molecule of glucose has the potential to form 38 molecules of ATP. Where oxygen is available, aerobic respiration achieves this maximum yield of ATP in three stages: **glycolysis**, the **tricarboxylic acid (TCA) cycle** and **oxidative phosphorylation**. Most of the ATP is formed in the third stage.

## 6.6 Glycolysis

In glycolysis, which takes place in the cytoplasm, the six-carbon glucose molecule is broken down into a three-carbon molecule known as **pyruvate**. As this is an oxidation process, a hydrogen carrier is needed. In glycolysis, this is NAD. Some of the early stages of glycolysis require energy; this is provided by ATP.

Figure 6.10 shows an outline of the main stages of glycolysis. The first

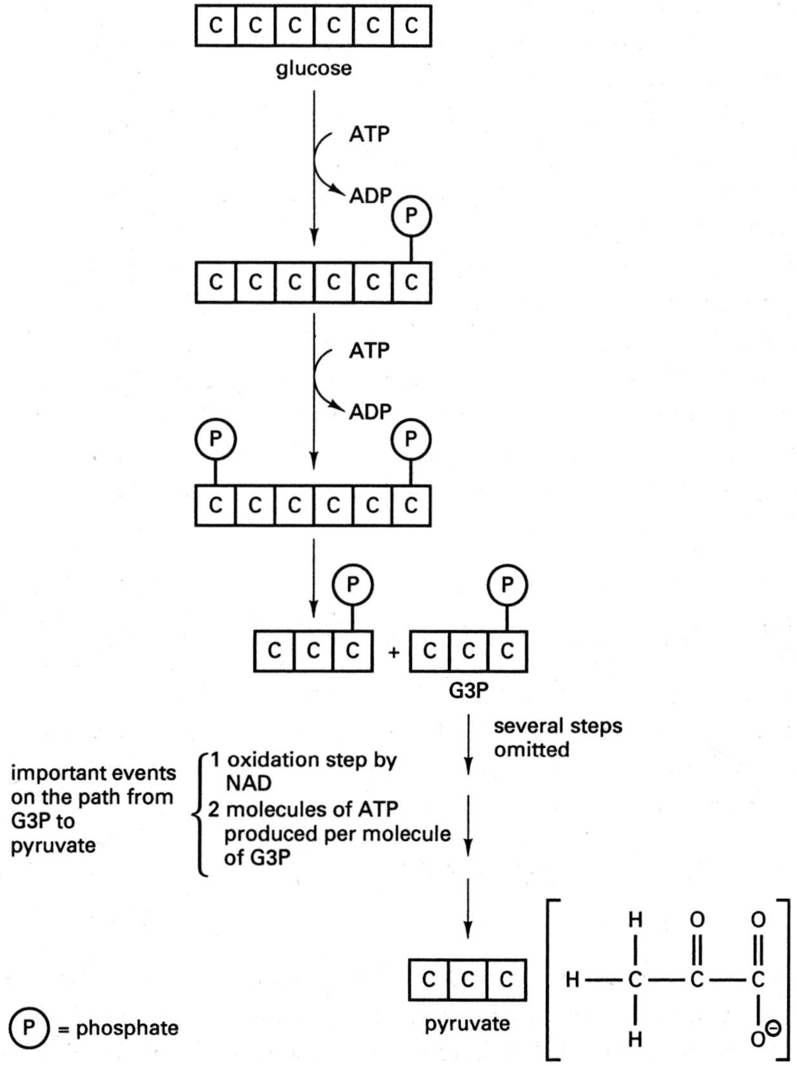

Figure 6.10 An outline of glycolysis.

important event is the formation of G3P (which was also an important metabolic intermediate in photosynthesis) from glucose. The energy of the glucose molecule is first increased by phosphorylation, which uses up two molecules of ATP. When it splits in two, it forms two isomeric three-carbon compounds, one of which is G3P. The isomer is readily converted into G3P, so we can simplify this stage by saying that each glucose molecule splits into two G3P molecules.

The next stage involves an oxidation step, where NAD removes a pair of hydrogen atoms, and two ATP molecules are released for each molecule of G3P that is turned into pyruvate.

The energy balance at the end of glycolysis is two ATP molecules for each molecule of glucose turned into pyruvate.

**QUESTION**   **12 Confirm this figure by checking Figure 6.10.**

### 6.7    The TCA cycle

The action now moves to the mitochondria. The first reaction is the formation of another key intermediate, **acetyl coenzyme A (acetyl-CoA)** from pyruvate by the following reaction:

$$\text{pyruvate} + \text{NAD}^+ + \text{CoA} \rightarrow \text{acetyl-CoA} + \text{CO}_2 + \text{NADH} + \text{H}^+$$

The pyruvate molecule splits into carbon dioxide and a two-carbon fragment known as the acetyl group. Coenzyme A (CoA) is a small molecule that carries the acetyl group into the first stage of the TCA cycle, where it combines with a four-carbon molecule called oxaloacetic acid to form **citric acid**. The rest of the

**Figure 6.11**

**Outline of the**

**TCA cycle.**

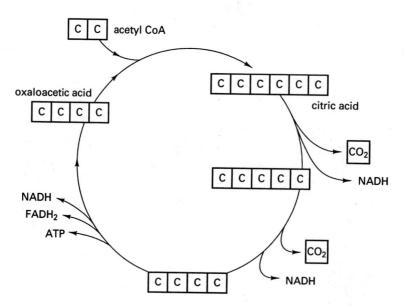

cycle consists of a progressive dismantling of the citric acid until two molecules of carbon dioxide are released. This leaves oxaloacetic acid ready to start another turn of the cycle (Figure 6.11). Three molecules of NADH and one of $FADH_2$ are produced in the TCA cycle, as well as one molecule of ATP for each molecule of acetyl-CoA that enters the cycle.

**13** At the end of the TCA cycle, what is the overall yield of ATP per molecule of glucose? What is the yield of reduced hydrogen carriers in the TCA cycle for each molecule of glucose entering glycolysis?

QUESTION

### 6.8 Oxidative phosphorylation

Most of the ATP available from glucose is released in the final stage of aerobic respiration. The key players in **oxidative phosphorylation** are the reduced hydrogen carriers, NADH and $FADH_2$, which were formed in the first two stages of respiration.

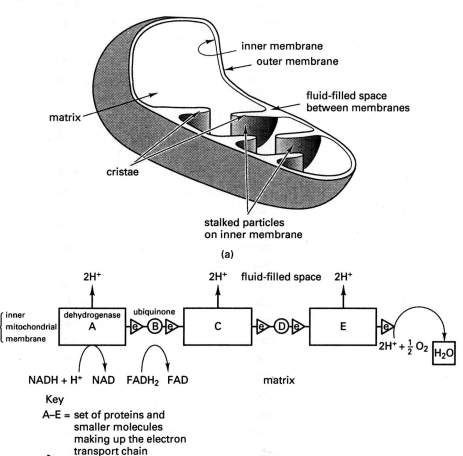

Figure 6.12 (a) The structure of a mitochondrion. (b) The electron transport chain.

The hydrogen carriers release protons and electrons to an **electron transport chain**. This is a set of proteins embedded in folds in the inner-mitochondrial membrane known as **cristae** (Figure 6.12a). Reduced NAD gives up its hydrogen atoms to a dehydrogenase enzyme; reduced FAD gives up its hydrogens to a coenzyme called ubiquinone (Figure 6.12b). This step regenerates the hydrogen carriers, ready to carry on their work in glycolysis and the TCA cycle.

Next, electrons are handed on to a group of proteins called the **cytochromes**. These contain **haem** as a prosthetic group. The iron atom in the haem is easily oxidised and reduced according to the following reaction:

$$Fe^{3+} + e^- \rightleftharpoons Fe^{2+}$$

As the electrons are handed on from one protein to the next, energy is released in stages. As in the light reaction of photosynthesis, this energy is used to pump protons, which pass into the fluid-filled spaces enclosed by the cristae. The electrons are finally handed on to an enzyme called **cytochrome oxidase**, which catalyses the formation of water from oxygen in the reaction:

$$2H^+ + 2e^- + \tfrac{1}{2}O_2 \rightarrow H_2O$$

The surface of the cristae is also studded with structures known as **stalked particles**. The enzyme **ATP synthase** is found within these stalked particles. The protons that have been pumped into the fluid-filled space flow back down the concentration gradient, through channels within the enzyme. As they do so, the enzyme is activated and forms ATP from ADP and phosphate. The amount of ATP produced depends upon the amount of NADH and $FADH_2$

**Table 6.1   Yields in the three stages of aerobic respiration (per molecule of glucose initially)**

| Stage | NADH/$FADH_2$ | ATP |
| --- | --- | --- |
| Glycolysis | $2 \times$ NADH | $2 \times$ ATP |
| TCA cycle | $8 \times$ NADH | $2 \times$ ATP |
|  | $2 \times FADH_2$ |  |
| Oxidative |  | $30 \times$ ATP |
|   phosphorylation* |  | $4 \times$ ATP |
| Totals | $10 \times$ NADH |  |
|  | $2 \times FADH_2$ | $38 \times$ ATP |

* In this step, each molecule of NADH gives three molecules of ATP, and each molecule of $FADH_2$ gives two molecules of ATP.

fed into the electron transport chain. Each molecule of NADH produces three of ATP, while each molecule of $FADH_2$ produces two molecules of ATP. So, 34 molecules of ATP for each glucose molecule broken down are available by this process (see Table 6.1).

QUESTIONS

14 How many molecules of reduced NAD and reduced FAD enter the electron transport chain for each molecule of glucose broken down? Does your answer confirm that oxidative phosphorylation produces 34 molecules of ATP?

15 What happens to the electron transport chain in the absence of oxygen?

16 What common features are there in the generation of ATP by photosynthesis and respiration?

17 Summarise the energy changes that take place in oxidative phosphorylation.

## Peter Mitchell and the chemiosmotic theory

The connection between the proton gradient across a membrane and the generation of ATP is one of the most powerful ideas in modern biology. It is known as the **chemiosmotic theory** and was developed by the British scientist Peter Mitchell, who died in 1992. Although Mitchell was rewarded for his work by a Nobel Prize in 1978, for many years he was ridiculed by fellow biologists, who could not accept his ideas.

The chemiosmotic theory gives us an insight into the energy transformations that occur in photosynthesis and respiration. Light energy from the Sun and chemical energy from glucose are both stored, temporarily, as electrochemical potential energy in the form of a proton gradient. This energy is easily transformed into ATP, but the structures of the thylakoid and inner mitochondrial membranes play a vital role in this.

The chemiosmotic theory gives us a new way of looking at membranes and enzymes. It shows the membrane as rather more than just a passive barrier, and enzymes as having a directional (Mitchell called it **vectorial**) quality when embedded in a membrane; the electron transport chain moves electrons in a given direction, for example, and protons flowing down the concentration gradient activate ATP synthase to resynthesise ATP.

Normally the proton gradient is used to make ATP, as the two processes are tightly coupled. But there are substances that act as uncouplers of oxidative phosphorylation. Like photosynthetic batteries, these substances work by tapping into the energy of the proton gradient. Hibernating animals, and animals that live in cold climates, use a protein known as thermogenin as an uncoupler – it can short-circuit the flow of protons, tapping the energy of the proton gradient as a source of heat. Similarly, the skunk cabbage uses heat generated in this way to warm its floral spikes, releasing the odours of volatile compounds to attract insects for pollination.

## 6.9   Alternative respiratory pathways

In the absence of oxygen, the electron transport chain closes down and **anaerobic respiration** takes over as a way of regenerating the NAD required to keep glycolysis going. Briefly, in anaerobic respiration pyruvic acid is diverted to the formation of lactic acid in mammals, and ethanol in yeast, as shown in Figure 6.13a. These reduction reactions produce NAD from NADH. Anaerobic respiration in microbes is often known as fermentation and is the source of many products with a commercial value, such as butanol and propanone, which are used as solvents, while ethanol is, of course, used to make alcoholic drinks.

The human body requires about 160 g of glucose a day – of which 120 g is needed by the brain. Glucose is stored as the polymer glycogen in the liver, and this is broken down when blood sugar (glucose) levels drop below 60 mg per 100 cm³. This breakdown is under the control of the hormones **glucagon** and **adrenaline**. When glycogen supplies are exhausted, a process known as gluconeogenesis takes over to top up glucose supplies.

In **gluconeogenesis**, fat, protein and lactate are converted into glucose as shown in outline in Figure 6.13b. Lipids are broken down by lipase enzymes to fatty acids and glycerol. The latter is converted into G3P, from which glucose is formed. Both amino acids, from the breakdown of protein, and lactate can be turned into pyruvate. A series of chemical reactions then create glucose from pyruvate.

Sugars other than glucose can also be metabolised. Fructose and galactose both enter glycolysis, but by different routes. One of the enzymes involved in the metabolism of galactose is missing in the autosomal recessive disease **galactosaemia**. Affected infants fail to thrive, suffering severe vomiting and

**Figure 6.13 (a) Anaerobic respiration. (b) An outline of gluconeogenesis.**

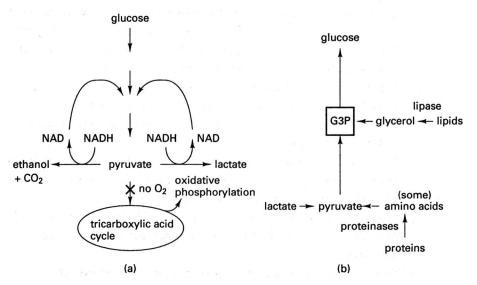

diarrhoea. If untreated, the disease leads to liver damage and mental retardation. Strict exclusion of galactose from the diet is the usual treatment.

18 What are the main sources of fructose and galactose in the diet?

19 Some people suffer from milk intolerance because they lack the enzyme lactase, which breaks down lactose. When lactose builds up in the intestine, it leads to cramps, nausea and diarrhoea. People suffering from milk intolerance can, however, usually digest milk products such as cheese and yoghurt. Why is this?

QUESTIONS

## Summary of Chapter 6

1  Photosynthesis builds up glucose from carbon dioxide in plants using the energy of sunlight.

2  Photosynthesis occurs in two stages – the light and dark reactions.

3  In the light reaction of photosynthesis, reduced NADP and ATP are synthesised and oxygen is produced from the photolysis of water.

4  In the dark reaction, G3P is produced from RBP and carbon dioxide. It is then reduced by NADPH to a triose sugar, from which glucose is synthesised.

5  Glucose is stored in the plant cell as cellulose, and as glycogen in animal cells. It is the primary substrate of respiration.

6  Energy in the form of ATP is extracted from glucose during respiration.

7  There are three stages of aerobic respiration – glycolysis, the TCA cycle and oxidative phosphorylation. The yields of NADH, $FADH_2$ and ATP for each stage (in molecules per molecule of glucose entering glycolysis) are given in Table 6.1.

8  The production of ATP during oxidative phosphorylation is linked to the generation of a proton gradient across the mitochondrial membrane, which arises from the oxidation of reduced NAD and FAD.

9  Oxygen is the final electron acceptor in aerobic respiration. In its absence, lactic acid or ethanol are produced from pyruvic acid by anaerobic respiration, which regenerates NAD.

10  Glucose is produced from glycogen when blood sugar levels fall, or from proteins or fats by gluconeogenesis in the absence of glycogen.

11  Sugars other than glucose can be metabolised by glycolysis.

## Examination questions

Figure 6.14

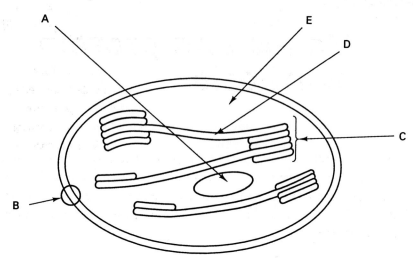

1   Copy Figure 6.14 which shows the structure of a chloroplast as seen with an electron microscope.
    (a)   (i) Name the features labelled A to E.
          (ii) Draw a circle round the value which best represents the magnification of the diagram
                $\times 150$        $\times 1500$        $\times 15\,000$        $\times 150\,000$
    (b)   (i) State the exact region of the chloroplast in which chlorophylls *a* and *b* would be found.
          (ii) Name one other pigment which might be found in a chloroplast from the leaf of a herbaceous flowering plant.
    (c)   Distinguish between the terms absorption spectrum and action spectrum. (WJEC, part of question)

2   'Living organisms can acquire and transform energy, using it to synthesise complex molecules.' Discuss this statement with reference to:
    (a)   The energy flow through an ecosystem.
    (b)   The electron transfer chain in a respiring cell.
    (c)   The light independent (dark) stage of photosynthesis. (WJEC)

3   Give an illustrated account of the structure of a mitochondrion.
    (b)   Describe how ATP is produced inside a mitochondrion.
    (c)   Outline the ways in which ATP is utilised in living organisms. (JMB, now NEAB, A/S)

4   Write an essay on ATP. (UCLES, S)

# chapter 7

# Genes and protein synthesis

As we have seen, cellular activities such as photosynthesis and respiration are under the control of enzymes. The enzymes themselves are built up from amino acids present in the cell into a precisely defined sequence by the actions of DNA and RNA. Errors in this process can have profound consequences for the whole organism.

## 7.1 The triplet code is the key to protein sequences

The sequence of bases in DNA specifies the order of amino acids in a protein sequence. But DNA remains in the nucleus, while proteins are synthesised in the cytoplasm. It is RNA that provides the physical link between DNA and proteins, and this is discussed in the next section. DNA provides, and passes on to the next generation, the information needed to assemble proteins in the correct order to work properly.

When Crick and Watson published their work on the structure of DNA, physicist George Gamow immediately began wondering how the order of the bases could be mapped onto an amino acid sequence. There are only four 'letters' in the DNA and RNA sequences, while the proteins that they synthesise have 20 amino acid 'letters'.

The bases had to code in small groups rather than as individuals – otherwise proteins could only have four different amino acids. Gamow founded a discussion group called the 'RNA Tie Club' for scientists who were interested in the problem of the genetic code. The Club suggested that the code was based upon non-overlapping groups of three bases. These sets of three were called **codons**. There are 64 possible codons – more than enough for the 20 amino acids, and some necessary 'punctuation' in the form of 'start' and 'stop' messages (Table 7.1). The start message is AUG, the codon for methionine. Note that this is an RNA code. It is RNA, rather than DNA, that is actually translated into proteins (this is discussed in more detail in the next section).

**Table 7.1　The base sequences of the triplet code and the amino acids for which they code**

| First base | Second base | | | | Third base |
|---|---|---|---|---|---|
| | U | C | A | G | |
| U | UUU ⎫ Phe<br>UUC ⎭<br>UUA ⎫ Leu<br>UUG ⎭ | UCU ⎫<br>UCC ⎪ Ser<br>UCA ⎪<br>UCG ⎭ | UAU ⎫ Tyr<br>UAC ⎭<br>UAA c.t.*<br>UAG c.t.* | UGU ⎫ Cys<br>UGC ⎭<br>UGA c.t.*<br>UGG Trp | U<br>C<br>A<br>G |
| C | CUU ⎫<br>CUC ⎪ Leu<br>CUA ⎪<br>CUG ⎭ | CCU ⎫<br>CCC ⎪ Pro<br>CCA ⎪<br>CCG ⎭ | CAU ⎫ His<br>CAC ⎭<br>CAA ⎫ Gln<br>CAG ⎭ | CGU ⎫<br>CGC ⎪ Arg<br>CGA ⎪<br>CGG ⎭ | U<br>C<br>A<br>G |
| A | AUU ⎫<br>AUC ⎬ Ile<br>AUA ⎭<br>AUG Met | ACU ⎫<br>ACC ⎪ Thr<br>ACA ⎪<br>ACG ⎭ | AAU ⎫ Asn<br>AAC ⎭<br>AAA ⎫ Lys<br>AAG ⎭ | AGU ⎫ Ser<br>AGC ⎭<br>AGA ⎫ Arg<br>AGG ⎭ | U<br>C<br>A<br>G |
| G | GUU ⎫<br>GUC ⎪ Val<br>GUA ⎪<br>GUG ⎭ | GCU ⎫<br>GCC ⎪ Ala<br>GCA ⎪<br>GCG ⎭ | GAU ⎫ Asp<br>GAC ⎭<br>GAA ⎫ Glu<br>GAG ⎭ | GGU ⎫<br>GGC ⎪ Gly<br>GGA ⎪<br>GGG ⎭ | U<br>C<br>A<br>G |

* c.t. = chain termination codon, equivalent to a full stop in the message.

**QUESTION**

1 Translate the following RNA sequence into a protein sequence:

　　AUGAAAGCUAAUGCUAAAACUAUUAUUGCU

2 How many codons would there be in a code based on (a) groups of two or (b) groups of four? Why are such arrangements not feasible for specifying protein sequences?

Experimental proof of the triplet code was provided by Marshall Nirenberg and Johann Matthaei in the early 1960s. Working with a form of

RNA known as poly-U, which is just a long chain of uracil-based nucleotides, they added this to 20 test tubes containing the enzymes and other substances known to be involved in protein synthesis and one out of the 20 amino acids. Only the test tube containing the amino acid phenylalanine gave any protein, and this consisted of a long string of phenylalanine residues. Similar experiments showed which codons corresponded to the rest of the amino acids, leading, by 1964, to the full genetic code.

**3 How would you use this experiment to show that AAA codes for lysine? How would you identify your product?**    QUESTION

The code appears to be universal; apart from a few exceptions, all organisms use it.

## 7.2    One gene codes for one polypeptide

The meaning of the word 'gene' has changed as biology has developed as a science. Gregor Mendel was the first to describe a gene as a unit of heredity, but he did not know what its physical nature was (nor did he actually use the term 'gene'). We now know that it is a stretch of DNA that codes for protein. This idea has grown from work carried out from 1941 onwards by George Beadle and E. L. Tatum. Using the pink fungus *Neurospora crassa*, which grows on bread, they investigated the effects of mutation on the metabolism of the fungi. Mutations – produced by exposing the fungi to X-rays – caused alterations in the microbes' ability to make certain substances needed for their growth. These mutant fungi could not grow on minimal medium – which contains everything the normal fungi needed for growth. However, if the substance they lacked was added to the medium, then they grew normally. For example, a mutant that cannot make histidine will grow on histidine-supplemented minimal medium. Mutants could be classified as to which supplements they needed in order to grow.

Beadle and Tatum argued that mutations were occurring in the genes that coded for the enzymes needed to synthesise the missing substance. They stated that one gene controlled the synthesis of one enzyme. This idea had already been put forward by Sir Archibald Garrod many years earlier when he was investigating the biochemical basis of human inherited disease. Beadle and Tatum put the '**one gene-one enzyme**' idea on a firm experimental footing and were rewarded with a Nobel Prize in 1958. Current views on the nature of the gene have modified Beadle and Tatum's original rule to '**one gene–one polypeptide**'.

**4 *Neurospora* has a haploid vegetative stage. Why was this an important feature of Beadle and Tatum's experiment? What other features of *Neurospora* might also have been important in the success of their work?**    QUESTION

**DNA directs the synthesis of protein through messenger RNA**

**Messenger RNA** (mRNA) is the link between DNA and protein. It carries a copy of the base sequence of a gene out of the nucleus to the ribosome, where the protein chain is assembled.

The process begins with a copying mechanism known as **transcription** (Figure 7.1). The enzyme **RNA polymerase** binds to the start codon of the gene and unwinds a section of DNA about 17 base pairs long by breaking the hydrogen bonds holding the two strands together. It then organises the assembly of a single strand of RNA complementary to one of the unwound DNA strands. This is the **template strand**. Apart from the substitution of T by U (since this is RNA), the base sequence of the mRNA is identical to the other DNA strand, which is known as the **coding strand**.

**Figure 7.1**

**Transcription.**

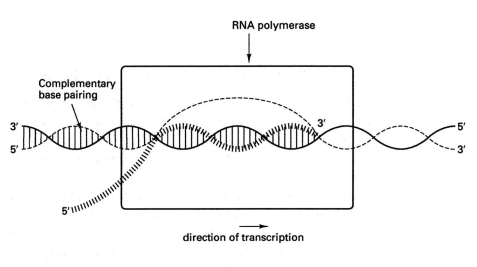

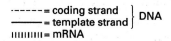

The temporary DNA–RNA helix unwinds as the RNA polymerase moves along the gene, continuing the assembly of the mRNA. The newly synthesised RNA is cast off as a single strand and the DNA double strand is rewound as the next section to be transcribed is unwound. The process is continuous, and synthesis of mRNA occurs from the 5′ to the 3′ end. When RNA polymerase reaches the stop codon on the gene, it becomes detached from the DNA, transcription terminates and the mRNA is then free to move out of the nucleus. (In bacteria, translation into protein may begin before transcription is complete.)

Some antibiotics and toxins work by interfering with transcription. Rifamycin, for example, stops the formation of the bond linking the first two nucleotides in bacterial mRNA. Actinomycin binds tightly to the DNA of both bacterial and cancer cells, stopping it from unwinding for transcription; this means that it is an effective antibiotic and anti-cancer drug. Finally, the mushroom *Amanita phalloides* is known as the 'death cap' or 'destroying angel' because it contains α-amanitin, a potent toxin. α-Amanitin binds tightly to RNA polymerase, effectively stopping transcription in human cells – resulting in more than a hundred deaths a year world-wide.

**5 Write down the mRNA corresponding to the following DNA coding strand:**    QUESTION
   **ATCGGGATACGT**
**6 Write down the mRNA corresponding to the following DNA template strand:**
   **GTGCATGACTGC**

### 7.4  Proteins are assembled on ribosomes

The ribosome is an organelle that is made up of **ribosomal RNA** (rRNA) and protein. It consists of a large and a small subunit. The latter locks on to a part of the mRNA sequence called the ribosome binding site. The whole ribosome then acts as a machine that assembles the protein chain in the order specified by the code carried on the mRNA, as shown in Figure 7.2.

The physical link between RNA and amino acids is **transfer RNA** (tRNA). Francis Crick envisaged the existence of tRNA several years before it was actually discovered. He called it the '**adaptor**' because this is its chemical function. tRNA contains the two features necessary to act as an 'adaptor': a triplet of bases called an **anticodon** that is complementary to a codon in mRNA, and a site where the amino acid specified by that codon can be attached. There is a whole set of tRNA molecules in the cytoplasm, corresponding to the 20 amino acids. So, for example, a tRNA for glycine could have the anticodon CCA because this is complementary to GGU, one of the glycine codons.

There are two tRNA binding sites on the ribosome. Close to the ribosome binding site on the mRNA is the start codon, AUG. tRNAs for methionine (the first amino acid) and the second amino acid assemble in the binding sites and base-pairing between the anticodons and the mRNA codons takes place, holding the tRNAs in place. An enzyme within the ribosome forms the first peptide bond, linking these two amino acids together.

The first tRNA then becomes detached from its amino acid, and the ribosome moves along to the next codon on the mRNA. The second tRNA takes the place of the first and the third tRNA moves into the adjacent tRNA binding site. The ribosome repeats the cycle and continues to move along the mRNA until the whole of the polypeptide chain has been synthesised. The chain is always synthesised from its N-terminus to its C-terminus.

**Figure 7.2 Stages in protein translation. (a) tRNAs, loaded with amino acids, move into position on the ribosome. (b) The first peptide bond is formed. (c) New loaded tRNA moves into position, unloaded tRNA moves off to collect another methionine molecule and the ribosome moves towards the 3' end of the mRNA.**

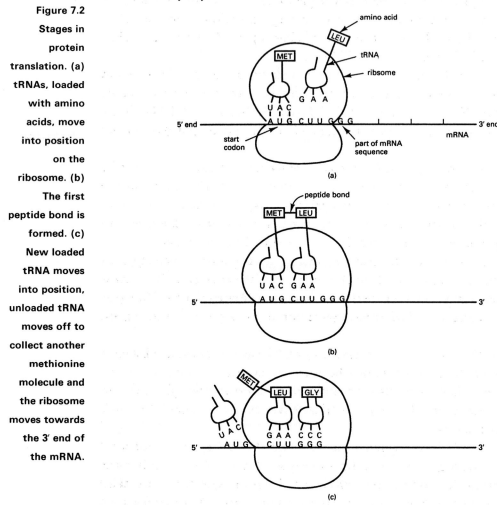

Many antibiotics work by blocking bacterial protein synthesis. For example, chloramphenicol interferes with the enzyme that links the amino acids together, while tetracycline binds to ribosomes, blocking the entry of the tRNA molecules.

**QUESTION** **7 Which anticodon(s) would be found on the tRNAs of the following amino acids: (a) phenylalanine, (b) lysine and (c) glutamic acid?**

###  7.5    A mutation in DNA may lead to a defective protein

Mutation is an alteration in the DNA sequence of a cell. Point mutations are single base-pair substitutions that occur during replication when the wrong base is inserted into the sequence as it is being copied. An example is when ATGGGGCCC becomes ATGGCGCCC.

Insertions or deletions of one or more base pairs can also occur, as can more extensive alterations such as deletions or rearrangements of whole segments of DNA. For example, if CCCTAGCGC becomes CCTAGCGC, a deletion has occurred; whereas if it becomes CGCCTAGCGC, an insertion has occurred.

Experiments with *Escherichia coli* have shown that the chance of a mistake occurring when one base pair replicates is about 1 in $10^4$. The actual mistake rate is closer to 1 in $10^{10}$. DNA polymerase possesses a powerful 'proof-reading' ability, which means that most mistakes are corrected. Bacteria with defective proof-reading enzymes show an increased mutation rate.

The mutation rate can be increased by certain chemicals – some of which are synthetic (such as vinyl chloride), others of which occur naturally (such as hydrazine in mushrooms). These chemicals are known as **mutagens**. Mutagens that cause cancer are called **carcinogens**; not all carcinogens are mutagens, however.

Table 7.2 lists some common carcinogens. The danger of these substances to human health depends upon the level of exposure. There are many thousands of other chemicals – both naturally occurring and synthetic – to which we are exposed every day that have not been tested for their carcinogenic potential.

Ultraviolet (UV) and gamma radiation are also mutagens, as are some viruses. UV damage is repaired by an enzyme that is defective in humans suffering from the skin disease xeroderma (from the Greek for dry skin) pigmentosa. Such individuals easily contract skin cancer and often die at an early age from complications of the disease.

Mutations that occur in germ-line cells (in humans, the sperm and egg) are passed on to future generations and are the cause of inherited diseases such as sickle cell anaemia, cystic fibrosis and haemophilia. Somatic cell mutations affect only the individual, and are not inherited.

**QUESTION**

8 Classify the 'mutations' in the following sentences and write some examples of your own:

(a) Ultraviolent light is a powerful mutagen.

(b) Paint mutations occur with higher than average frequency at certain sites on the genome.

(c) The roof-reading enzyme activity of DNA polymerase is crucial to the cell's survival.

**Table 7.2   Substances (and processes) agreed by the International Agency for Research into Cancer to be human carcinogens. This is a selection of the 50 chemicals in this category**

Nickel and its compounds

Arsenic and its compounds

Chromium compounds

Aflatoxins (toxins produced by *Aspergillus* fungi, which commonly grow on peanuts and rice)

Coal tar

Tobacco smoke

The rubber industry

Asbestos

Vinyl chloride (the chemical from which polyvinyl chloride – PVC – is made)

## Effect of point mutations on proteins

When it comes to transcription of a gene with a point mutation, the mutation is copied along with the rest of the sequence. The effect on the protein synthesised from the mRNA depends upon which codon carries the mutation.

The **degeneracy** of the genetic code ensures that many mutations are **silent** and have no effect on polypeptide sequence. For example, if GAA is mutated into GAG the amino acid coded for is still glutamic acid. But in sickle cell anaemia, a GAA codon in the globin gene is mutated into GUA. This results in the substitution of valine for glutamic acid and is an example of a **missense** mutation – one that changes the amino acid sequence of a polypeptide. Although such altered proteins may still have full biological activity, the haemoglobin resulting from this particular mutation is severely defective (see Chapter 2).

Some point mutations result in the formation of a stop codon. These are called **nonsense** mutations. If, for example, UAC (which codes for tyrosine) becomes UAA, protein synthesis will terminate at this point on the mRNA instead of inserting a tyrosine residue. Such a protein is likely to be non-functional.

QUESTION   **9 By making single base changes, introduce (a) a silent mutation, (b) a missense mutation and (c) a nonsense mutation into the codon AAA (refer to Table 7.1).**

## Gene expression is determined by proteins

Every cell in an organism contains the same DNA, but only certain genes are active in cells of any one type. When genes are transcribed and translated, they are said to be **expressed**. For example, the human insulin gene is only expressed in pancreatic cells, although it is present in all the other cells of the body. There must be some way in which gene expression can be turned on and off to account for this cellular specificity.

Much of our understanding of how genes are controlled comes from work done in the 1960s by Jacques Monod and Francois Jacob using *E. coli*. Like other bacteria, *E. coli* has an economical and adaptable life-style. Although it can live on lactose as a carbon and energy source if necessary, it needs to synthesise the enzyme β-galactosidase to do so. Thousands of molecules of β-galactosidase are present in *E. coli* cells when they are growing on lactose. But when it grows on other carbon sources, such as glucose, it does not waste resources synthesising β-galactosidase that is not going to be used; fewer than ten molecules of the enzyme are found in *E. coli* cells under these conditions.

Clearly the gene coding for β-galactosidase is switched on in the presence of lactose and off in its absence. The enzyme is said to be **inducible**, because its synthesis from the gene can be induced by the presence of certain substances, known as inducers. Inducers may be the substances whose reactions are catalysed by the enzyme (its substrate) or closely related compounds. Enzymes that are not inducible are known as **constitutive enzymes** – they are synthesised all the time.

In an elegant series of experiments involving mutants of *E. coli*, Monod and Jacob showed that *E. coli* has a gene that codes for a protein known as a **repressor protein**, which regulates the expression of the β-galactosidase gene. In the model that they proposed, this protein binds to a non-coding region of DNA known as the **operator**. The operator is next to another region of non-coding DNA called the **promoter**, where RNA polymerase binds prior to transcription (Figure 7.3). With the repressor protein in position, RNA polymerase cannot gain access to the promoter and transcription does not take place. The repressor protein is acting as an 'off' switch.

When the inducer, a compound closely related to lactose and formed from it, is present in the cell, it binds to the repressor. This binding alters the shape of the protein so that it no longer has any affinity for the operator and diffuses away. RNA polymerase is no longer prevented access to the operator and transcription of the β-galactosidase and other genes needed for the metabolism of lactose begins.

Jacob and Monod called the stretch of DNA that includes the promoter, the operator and the coding regions (two other enzymes are coded for besides β-galactosidase) the **lac operon**. They were awarded the Nobel Prize for this concept in 1965.

Gene control in eukaryotes is more complicated, but they also have promoter regions and DNA-binding proteins that act as molecular switches, turning transcription on and off.

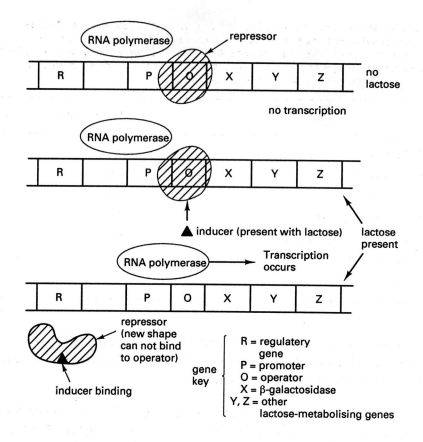

**Figure 7.3 The lac operon.**

QUESTION　**10 A mutant *E. coli* was found to contain a high concentration of β-galactosidase when grown on glycerol. In which gene would you expect to find this mutation? Another mutant *E. coli* cannot metabolise lactose. Which gene might be mutated in this second mutant?**

## 7.6　Reading the book of humanity: the Human Genome Project

Humans have 50 000 to 100 000 genes in their genome. These are spread among our 46 chromosomes (22 pairs, and the X and Y chromosomes). We know the location of about 2000 of these genes. Most of this information has come from studying the genomes of families with inherited diseases whose genes for these proteins are mutated from the normal sequence. Some examples are given in Table 7.3.

**Table 7.3 Genes for proteins involved in inherited diseases and their chromosomal location. (Note: genes are sometimes named after the disease with which they are associated, rather than the protein for which they code; so the gene for CFTR protein, which is defective in cystic fibrosis, is called the cystic fibrosis gene)**

| Gene | Chromosomal location |
| --- | --- |
| Cystic fibrosis | 7 |
| Sickle cell anaemia | 11 |
| Phenylketonuria | 12 |
| Osteogenesis imperfecta | 17 |
| Familial hypercholesterolaemia | 19 |
| Muscular dystrophy | X |
| Haemophilia | X |

**11 Can you name and describe the function of the proteins that are defective in the conditions named in Table 7.3? (Hint: all of these have been discussed in earlier chapters.)**

QUESTION

In 1988, the international scientific community, led by the United States, decided that it was time to coordinate the search for human genes. The **Human Genome Project** (HUGO for short) was set up under the leadership of James Watson (the co-discoverer of the DNA structure). The aims of HUGO are two-fold: to explore the 'geography' of the genome and map all the genes onto their chromosomes, and to work out the base sequence of the entire genome.

**12 There are $3 \times 10^9$ base pairs in the human genome and (say) 100 000 genes. If one gene is about 1000 base pairs, what percentage of the human genome actually codes for protein?**

QUESTION

No one knows the function of the non-coding regions of DNA; for this reason it is sometimes called '**junk**' or '**selfish**' DNA – the latter name arises from the fact that it replicates yet does not (apparently) contribute anything to the organism.

Given a long DNA sequence, it is actually quite easy for a computer to sort out coding from non-coding DNA and to find genes within 'junk' DNA. Coding regions are known as **open-reading frames** (ORFs) and they are long stretches of sequence without stop codons. In non-coding DNA there would be a stop codon about every 60 bases (there are three stop codons out of the 64 in the genetic code). In a gene, there are about 1000 bases before the stop codon.

**QUESTION 13 Two DNA sequences are shown below. One is part of the gene that codes for the enzymes that synthesise the amino acid tryptophan in *E. coli*; the other is a non-coding sequence. Identify which sequence is the gene.**

**(a) ATGCAAACCGTTTTAGCGAAAGTCGCAGACAAGGCGATTTGGGTA GAAGCCCGCAAA CAGCAGCAACCGCTGGCCAGTTTTCAG**

**(b) GTTTAACGTAGAGGGGGAGATTGTCTACTGAAAACACCGCCTTGT AGATTTCTCCAGAAACCGATACTCCACGCCGGTTAATCA**

The DNA of humans and other eukaryotes is further complicated by the fact that genes themselves are interrupted by non-coding regions known as **introns**. The coding regions are called **exons**. mRNA copies the whole gene, then loops out the introns – an example of the catalytic activity of RNA.

Sequencing the human genome is a huge task. To date, only viruses have had their whole genome sequenced – the largest being that of cytomegalovirus at 250 000 base pairs. Naturally, the genome of *E. coli* has come under scrutiny, but only about a fifth of its genome has been sequenced.

**DNA sequencing** was pioneered by Frederick Sanger, the British scientist who worked out the sequence of insulin. His DNA work won him a second Nobel Prize for Chemistry, in 1980. Sequencing, which uses radio-labelling of the phosphorus in DNA coupled with various chemical methods of breaking the molecule into smaller pieces, is now a fully automated process.

The HUGO team says that the map of the human genome will be completed by the end of the century. The sequencing will take a little longer – maybe 15 years. To make sense of the human data, it is important to have information about the genomes of other species. Teams working on the genomes of the pig, the mouse, *Arabidopsis thaliana* (a type of cress), the fruit fly and the worm *Caenorhabditis elegans* are cooperating closely with the HUGO project. Sharing this information will give new insights into the unity and divergence of living organisms.

Watson said recently 'Getting the human genes . . . is the most important thing in biology.' Not all scientists agree – some think it will divert cash from other pressing research problems, while others worry that human genome data could be misused. Whatever the outcome, HUGO will change our lives. It will be as if we were handed the instruction booklet to our bodies and with it a knowledge of our strengths and weaknesses. While this knowledge could help us to plan happier and more productive lives, it could also be difficult to handle if it affects our employment prospects or our ability to have a healthy family. The diseases listed in Table 7.3 are relatively rare. HUGO is likely to provide information about more common conditions such as high blood pressure, heart disease, cancer, alcoholism and mental illness.

14 Working in groups, imagine that a complete sequence of your genome **QUESTION**
with a map of your genes is available. Discuss this from the point of
view of: (a) a couple planning a family; (b) a potential employer; (c) an
insurance company; (d) yourself planning a diet (not necessarily a
slimming diet); and (e) any other point of view that seems relevant to
you.

## Summary of Chapter 7

1   The DNA code for protein is a triplet code. Genes are coded as
triplets called codons, which correspond to the 20 amino acids
and include three stop codons to mark the end of the genes.

2   mRNA is the link between DNA and protein. It copies a gene
during the transcription process with the help of the enzyme
RNA polymerase and passes out of the nucleus to the ribosome.

3   mRNA binds to the ribosome and its codons pair with anticodons
on tRNAs that carry the amino acids specified by the codons. An
enzyme in the ribosome forms peptide bonds between the amino
acids, forming a polypeptide chain.

4   Mutations in the DNA coding sequence can lead to defective
proteins and inherited diseases. Most mutations are repaired by
DNA polymerase, however. The frequency of mutation is
increased by some chemicals, ultraviolet light and some viruses.

5   The Human Genome Project will locate all the genes to their
chromosomal position, providing a complete map, which will
give much useful information about our inherited characteristics
and our susceptibility to disease.

## Examination questions

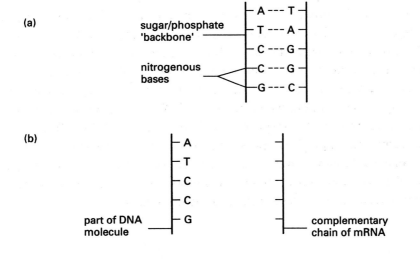

Figure 7.4

1   Figure 7.4a shows a portion of a DNA molecule.
    (a)  Show with the help of diagrams how this portion replicates.
    (b)  (i)  Copy and complete Figure 7.4b to show the base
             sequence which would result when a complementary
             chain of messenger RNA is produced.
        (ii)  What is the function of the base sequence of mRNA?
             (London)

2   Write an essay on gene expression, including reference to animal
    and plant examples where appropriate. (London)

3   The following are combined in a flask in a suitable medium:
    • ribosomes extracted from rat's livers
    • myoglobin messenger RNA molecules extracted from beef
    • tRNA extracted from a culture of yeast
    • energy-rich compounds such as ATP and GTP, extracted from
      yeast
    • all the necessary ions
    • the protein factors required for the various phases of protein
      synthesis
    (a)  What elements have to be added to the mixture in order to
         achieve protein synthesis in the flask? If they are added, what
         protein will be synthesised? Justify your answers.
    (b)  Using diagrams, explain the mechanism of this synthesis. (IB,
         Higher Level)

4.  (a)  Explain what is meant by the term 'nucleotide'.
    (b)  Describe, with the aid of diagrams, the functions of the
         various forms of nucleic acids in protein synthesis. (JMB,
         now NEAB, A/S)

# chapter 8

# DNA technology

The discovery of the structure of DNA revealed the molecular nature of the gene. It also led to the development of powerful new technologies such as genetic engineering and DNA fingerprinting. DNA technology is already having a great impact in medicine, agriculture and industry.

## 8.1 Genes can be transferred between species by genetic engineering

Several human proteins, such as insulin and growth hormone, are now produced in fermenters. There are plants that contain genes to protect them from insects, and sheep that produce human blood-clotting proteins in their milk. These are just a few products of **genetic engineering**, a set of techniques in which genes from one species are transferred to another species through the action of **restriction enzymes** – sometimes also known as **restriction endonucleases**.

Restriction enzymes are extracted from bacteria, which use them to chop up the DNA of invading viruses. Each restriction enzyme acts like a pair of molecular scissors, cutting DNA at a specific target sequence. Their names contain three-letter abbreviations for the species from which they come, e.g. EcoRI comes from *Escherichia coli*. Over 300 restriction enzymes have now been purified. Some restriction enzymes, such as BamHI, cut DNA to leave unpaired or **'sticky' ends** at the site of the cut. Others – HaeIII for example – cut the DNA leaving **'blunt' ends**. Some examples are shown in Table 8.1.

**1 Use Table 8.1 to show the fragments produced when (a) EcoRI and (b) HaeIII act on the DNA sequences shown, labelling the sticky and blunt ends.**

QUESTION

Genetic engineering occurs in the following four key stages (see Figure 8.1 on page 115):

1   Isolation of the gene to be transferred.
2   Insertion of the gene into a vector.
3   Transfer of the gene to the host cell and selection of transformed cells.
4   Multiplication of the host cells in a fermenter to produce the protein for which the transferred gene codes.

**Table 8.1   Restriction enzymes (∗ shows point where enzyme cuts). Only a small part of the whole DNA molecule is shown in each case here**

| | |
|---|---|
| BamHI | G∗GATCC |
| | CCTAG∗G |
| EcoRI | G∗AATTC |
| | CTTAA∗G |
| HaeIII | GG∗CC |
| | CC∗GG |

## Isolation of the gene to be transferred (stage 1)

The gene to be transferred is isolated from the rest of the DNA in the cell. One method of doing this is based upon the mRNA for the gene.

(a) Cells that express the gene of interest will contain its mRNA, which can be isolated. The enzyme **reverse transcriptase** will catalyse the copying of a **complementary DNA** (cDNA) strand onto this mRNA.

(b) The RNA can then be degraded with alkali, leaving a single cDNA strand.

(c) Another enzyme, **DNA polymerase**, now catalyses the formation of a second DNA strand, resulting in copies of the gene of interest.

(d) Alternatively, if the DNA sequence of the gene is known, a synthetic gene can be produced by linking nucleotides together in the correct order on an automated DNA synthesiser.

## Insertion of the gene into a vector (stage 2)

The isolated gene cannot usually be transferred directly into the host cell. (Note that Griffith's experiments, described in Chapter 3, were a rare exception to this rule.) It must be carried in by a **vector**. Vectors are naturally occurring sequences of DNA that can be cut open by restriction enzymes, so that the target gene DNA can be inserted.

One common vector used in genetic engineering is the **plasmid**. This is a circle of DNA that occurs naturally in bacteria and yeast. Plasmids contain their own genes – often these code for proteins that help the microbe to resist antibiotics. They are transferred easily from one bacterium to another. This makes them ideal vehicles for carrying genes into bacterial cells because they naturally invade such cells. The gene is inserted into the plasmid as follows.

(a) The plasmid is first cut by a restriction enzyme. As we have seen, this may leave sticky or blunt ends, depending on the enzyme used. In Figure 8.1 only sticky ends will be considered.

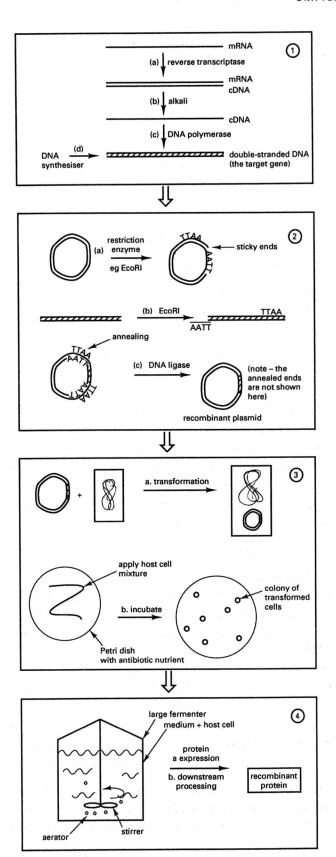

Figure 8.1
Outline of key
stages in
genetic
engineering.

(b) The gene is treated with the same restriction enzyme.

(c) Now gene and vector have complementary ends. When they are mixed together, they join up, or anneal, by base-pairing. Another enzyme, **DNA ligase**, completes the seal by bonding the phosphate backbone together.

It is not always possible to find a restriction enzyme that produces sticky ends in the gene and the vector. If blunt ends need to be joined together, another enzyme can be used to attach artificial sticky ends. For example, if an AAAAA tail is attached to the plasmid blunt ends, and a complementary TTTTT tail to the ends of the gene, these will quickly hydrogen bond and can then be sealed by the ligase.

Sometimes a **bacteriophage** (a virus that infects bacteria) is used as a vector. DNA is inserted into the bacteriophage in the same way as for the plasmid.

The DNA of the vectors is now known as **recombinant DNA** because it contains DNA that is foreign to it. This DNA combination does not occur in Nature.

## Transfer of the gene to the host cell and selection of transformed cells (stage 3)

(a) The vector is now allowed to infect the host cell. Where the vector is a plasmid, this process is known as **transformation**; if it is a bacteriophage, it is called **transfection**. Here, *E. coli* is used as the host cell; in practice, a very wide range of cells may be used. It depends on the nature of the gene – sometimes it is more appropriate to use mammalian or plant cells as hosts.

(b) Not all the host cells take up the vector. It would be a waste of resources to grow these cells as they do not contain the required gene. Selection at this stage is an important part of the process. The plasmid usually has antibiotic resistance genes. If we grow a sample of host cells on a medium containing an appropriate antibiotic (e.g. chloramphenicol), only the transformed cells will grow.

## Multiplication of the host cells in a fermenter to produce the protein for which the transferred gene codes (stage 4)

(a) Colonies of transformed cells are grown on under suitable conditions of nutrient, pH and temperature in a sterile large-scale fermenter.

(b) The transferred gene is expressed along with those of the host cell. The recombinant protein is isolated from the fermentation medium by a variety of separation processes in a stage known as downstream processing – the cells may have to be broken open, or the protein may be precipitated directly from the fermentation medium. The details of downstream processing depend on the nature of the protein and the host cell.

The main aim of this type of genetic engineering has been to produce human proteins. This is useful in cases where the natural source of the protein is prone to contamination. For instance, in the early 1980s many haemophiliacs contracted AIDS after treatment with Factor VIII, a blood-clotting protein, that had been extracted from HIV-contaminated human plasma.

*E. coli* is not always an ideal host for human genes, however. Many human proteins need to be tagged with carbohydrate molecules for full biological activity. Prokaryotes are not able to carry out this **glycosylation** step, so eukaryotic hosts such as yeast or mammalian cells are used to make these glycoproteins. Some genetically engineered human proteins are shown in Table 8.2.

**2** The following account of the production of genetically engineered human insulin appeared in a Sunday newspaper:

    'Human insulin isn't actually taken from humans. It starts out as pork insulin or yeast bacteria and, through enzyme modification or genetic engineering, comes to have exactly the same DNA as ordinary human insulin.'

    How many mistakes can you find? Now rewrite it correctly, using roughly the same number of words.

**QUESTION**

**Table 8.2 Genetically engineered human proteins (CHO cells are Chinese hamster ovary cells)**

| Protein | Host cell | Use |
| --- | --- | --- |
| Insulin | *E. coli* | diabetes |
| Growth hormone | *E. coli* | dwarfism |
| Interferon | *E. coli* | cancer therapy |
| α-1 Antitrypsin | yeast | emphysema |
| Hepatitis B antigen | yeast | vaccine |
| Factor VIII | yeast | haemophilia |
| Tissue plasminogen activator | CHO | thrombosis |
| Erythropoietin | CHO | anaemia |
| Haemoglobin | yeast | severe blood loss |

### 8.2   Genetic engineering creates transgenic plants

Plants have been modified by conventional breeding methods for thousands of years; genetic engineering adds a new dimension to this tradition. Plants containing foreign genes – **transgenic plants** – are created in two stages. First, the foreign genes are transferred to the host plant cells – a process known as **transformation**. Then the transformed cells are grown into plants by plant tissue culture. This second stage is called **regeneration**.

## Plant cells can be transformed by *Agrobacterium tumefaciens*

The bacterium *Agrobacterium tumefaciens* is a natural genetic engineer. It infects a wide range of plant species by transferring a plasmid containing some of its own genes to the plant cells. These transferred genes stimulate the production of plant hormones, which cause the plant to form tumour-like tissue that the bacteria colonise. The infection is known as crown gall disease.

*A. tumefaciens* has been used to transfer new genes into many plants (Figure 8.2). One way of doing this involves making discs of leaf tissue with an ordinary hole punch and soaking these in a culture of *Agrobacterium* containing the desired gene on its plasmid. Tobacco, potato and petunia are particularly easy to transform in this way, and have acted as the pioneering species of plant genetic engineering.

## Protoplasts and whole plant cells take up DNA molecules

*Agrobacterium* infects broad-leaved plants more easily than it does cereals. Biotechnologists are particularly interested in adding new genes to cereals such as rice, corn and wheat, and have been looking at other gene transfer methods.

The plant cell wall forms a natural barrier to the uptake of DNA. However, if it is stripped away by the enzyme cellulase, **protoplasts** are formed, which can soak up DNA more easily. It can be carried through the cell membrane on polyethylene glycol (PEG) molecules, or the cells can be given a sudden electric shock, which causes small pores to open in the membrane through which the DNA can pass into the cells. Figure 8.2 shows a third method of transferring DNA into cells, without removing their walls. Tiny particles of gold or tungsten are coated with DNA and 'shot' into the plant with a particle gun. The shooting does not harm the plant – the holes in the cell walls made by the particles close up spontaneously.

**QUESTION    3 Draw diagrams to illustrate the transformation of rice protoplasts.**

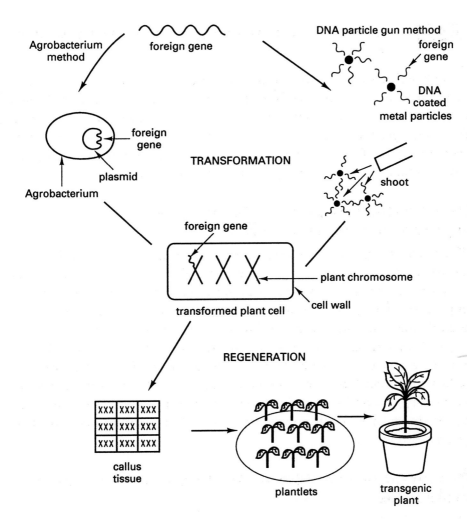

Figure 8.2
Creation of
transgenic
plants by
genetic
engineering.

## Transgenic plants offer new possibilities for disease and weed control

By the turn of the century, world population will be about 6 billion. To meet the growing demands on global food supplies, we need to look at new ways of preventing crop losses to pests, disease, weeds and drought.

One of the first goals of plant genetic engineering was the creation of pest-resistant plants. Important crops such as cotton, potato and corn can be protected from insect attack by the insertion of a gene for an insect toxin. This toxin is a protein that is made by the bacterium *Bacillus thuringiensis* (bt). It is specific to the caterpillars of moth and butterfly pests and attacks them by punching holes in their gut. It has no effect on other species. Gardeners and farmers have already been using bt proteins as insecticides for some years. The problem is that they break down easily and have to be reapplied at frequent intervals. The alternatives are more toxic substances, which may contaminate soil and ground water.

Transgenic plants have been made that contain the bt gene. They manufacture the bt insecticide continuously, avoiding the costs of repeated external applications. The bt gene in cotton plants – a major cash crop – offered complete protection from caterpillar damage, and field trials of transgenic potatoes and maize with the bt gene also demonstrate their immunity to attack by beetles.

Weeds are the other big threat to crop yields. Chemical herbicides are effective, but have the drawback that they often kill crop plants as well as weeds. Like pesticides, some of them also contaminate the environment. One herbicide, glyphosate, blocks an enzyme called EPSP, which plants need for growth. A gene for a different version of EPSP that is insensitive to glyphosate has been transferred to tomato, soybean and cotton. Field tests have shown that these plants remain unaffected, while glyphosate kills the surrounding weeds.

German scientists have recently shown that it is possible to engineer two useful functions into a plant with just one gene. They have transferred a gene to experimental tobacco plants that codes for an enzyme which destroys the herbicide cyanamide. The cyanamide is broken down by this enzyme to urea, which acts as a natural fertiliser for the plant. It should be possible to transfer this enzyme to important crop plants.

QUESTION   **4 What property of plants makes them natural candidates for genetic engineering?**

## Genetic engineering offers novel foods, plants and other products

Another approach to making transgenic plants is to turn off some of its genes instead of adding new ones. This can be done by introducing a so-called **'anti-sense'** version of a gene into the plant cells. This is a single strand of DNA with a sequence complementary to that of the mRNA of the target gene. It binds to the mRNA and stops it from leaving the nucleus, effectively turning off gene expression.

Tomatoes have had anti-sense genes inserted into their cells that can turn off the genes which control the ripening process. These tomatoes stay firm and do not turn soft and squashy on storage. The transgenic tomatoes have not yet reached the shops, but the anti-sense technique could one day save large amounts of fruit from tropical countries from rotting before it reaches the consumer.

Anti-sense technology has also been used to create new flower colours. By turning off flower colour genes, Dutch plant scientists have turned brightly coloured petunias into pale versions, some with unusual patterns on their petals.

Plants could also be used as factories in the same way as *E. coli* is used in the manufacture of insulin. One plan is to transfer the bacterial genes for polyhydroxybutyrate (Biopol, the biodegradable plastic) to potatoes so that they could produce the plastic instead of starch in their tubers. Other projects include transgenic sunflowers containing the gene for ricinoleic acid – a petroleum alternative for the chemical industry – and plants that can manufacture human antibodies.

## Genetic engineering has stimulated research into basic plant biology

We still know very little about plant biology. Genetic engineering targets such as enhancing photosynthetic ability or transferring the genes for nitrogen fixation will not be realised in the near future, if ever.

The prospect of global warming has led to an interest in searching out the genes that lead to salt and drought tolerance, in the hope that they may one day be transferred to important crops to enable them to survive in a hotter world. The mapping of the *Arabidopsis* genome is likely to pinpoint many of these genes.

**QUESTION**

5 **Suppose you have been working with kalar grass, a plant grown by Pakistani farmers in highly saline soils as a food for their livestock. You have just discovered a gene that gives kalar grass its salt resistance. Outline how you would attempt to create transgenic wheat plants containing this gene. Who would benefit from these plants? Who would have an interest in your research?**

**8.3    Transgenic animals make human proteins**

It is more difficult to make transgenic animals than transgenic plants, as animals are not totipotent. This means that the new genes must be introduced into the fertilised egg by a **micro-injection** technique. Research on mice has shown that only a few of the mice injected with foreign DNA actually incorporate it into their genome. However, it has been possible to produce 'supermice', which are twice the normal size, by introducing the gene for human growth hormone. This is important because it shows that mice can express human genes.

Pigs, sheep, goats and cows have all been given human genes. The aim is to have the animals produce the human protein in their milk. These farm animals have, so far, been able to produce haemoglobin, **Factor IX**, a blood-clotting protein, and **α-1 antitrypsin**, which helps to control the activity of enzymes known as proteases. It is probable that α-1 antitrypsin will be the first protein to be made in animals on a commercial basis. Researchers in Edinburgh expect to be producing 1000 kg of protein a year from a flock of 1000 sheep by 1995. Some people inherit an α-1 antitrypsin deficiency, with the result that their lung tissue is destroyed by the unrestrained action of one particular protease known as elastase. Homozygotes for α-1 antitrypsin deficiency suffer from the lung disease **emphysema**, in which the alveoli lose their elasticity, as elastase degrades elastic fibres and connective tissue proteins. Heterozygotes who smoke are in danger of developing the disease because the smoke oxidises a crucial methionine residue in α-1 antitrypsin, making it non-functional. There is a world market of thousands of kilograms for α-1 antitrypsin to be used as therapy for emphysema sufferers. Traditionally, it has been extracted from plasma at a concentration of only $2 \, g \, l^{-1}$. The transgenic sheep in Edinburgh promise to meet this demand with a yield of $35 \, g \, l^{-1}$.

**QUESTION**    **6 How could human proteins be isolated from the milk of transgenic animals?**

 **8.4** **DNA technology opens up new possibilities in medicine**

## Probing with DNA

Once a gene has been sequenced, **DNA probes**, which match it by complementary base-pairing, can be synthesised and used to pick that gene out of the rest of the genome. The general method for doing this is illustrated in Figure 8.3.

First, DNA is extracted from a small sample of blood, saliva, skin or other biological material. This is done either by hand or by an automated DNA extractor. The DNA is then incubated with a mixture of restriction enzymes, which chops it up into a set of more manageable fragments.

These fragments are now separated by electrophoresis. A set of DNA fragments of known length is run alongside the sample as a control so that the length of the sample fragments can be measured.

The sample and control are then denatured by treatment with alkali and the single-stranded DNA is transferred to a nylon membrane. So far, all the bands are completely invisible. The membrane is then incubated with a DNA sequence complementary to the gene of interest. Note that it is not necessary for the whole of the gene sequence to be present in the probe – a sample of the sequence of 10–20 base pairs is sufficient. The probe must be labelled in some way – with a radioactive or fluorescent tag, for example.

During the incubation, the probe binds by complementary base-pairing to the gene. After washing, the membrane is exposed to photographic paper or to ultraviolet light to detect the probe. Only the band(s) containing the gene sequence will light up.

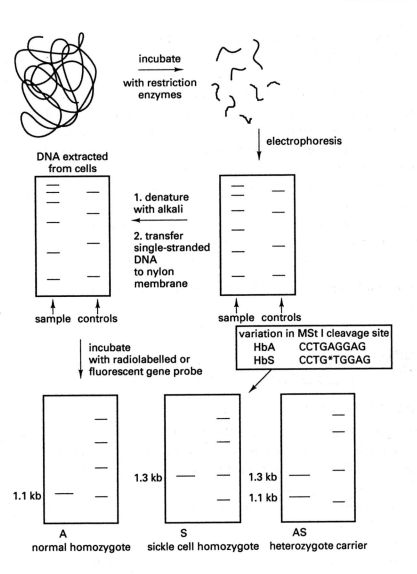

**Figure 8.3 Use of a DNA probe in the diagnosis of sickle cell anaemia.**

Figure 8.3 shows how the technique works in the detection of sickle cell anaemia. The gene of interest here is the β-globin gene, so the probe is a sequence from this gene. The mutation in sickle cell anaemia occurs in the cleavage site of the restriction enzyme MstII. So we would expect a longer β- globin fragment for the abnormal (S) globin gene as MstII is no longer able to cleave DNA at this point. The fragment concerned has a length of 1.3 kb, while the normal (A) globin gene, which does cleave at this site, gives a 1.1 kb fragment. This gives quite distinct patterns for homozygous normals (1.1 kb only), homozygous sickle cell anaemia (1.3 kb only) and heterozygotes (1.1 and 1.3 kb bands).

The overall technique is known as **Southern blotting** after E. M. Southern, who devised it. There are many variations, depending on the nature of the gene under investigation.

The technique is used as an aid to genetic counselling for couples planning a family who may be carriers of or sufferers from diseases whose genes have been identified. Examples of such diseases include haemophilia, muscular dystrophy, cystic fibrosis and thalassaemia. Once the carrier status of the couple is established, the chances of having an affected child can be discussed with them.

DNA probes can also be used for prenatal diagnosis using tissue from the foetus. Since the development of PCR (the polymerase chain reaction, discussed in Chapter 3), tiny tissue samples can be taken and amplified at a very early stage of pregnancy – giving the parents more time to consider their options if the child is found to be affected.

## DNA fingerprinting

Southern blotting can also be used in DNA fingerprinting – a technique devised to establish an individual's identity, rather than to detect the presence of inherited disease.

We all have genomes that differ in sequence (except for identical twins). Many of these differences can be picked up by restriction enzymes because they abolish or create restriction sites. These differences are called **restriction fragment length polymorphisms** (RFLPs) because they change the length of restriction fragments. This means that each individual's DNA produces a different set of fragments when incubated with a set of restriction enzymes.

In a DNA fingerprint, these are probed by a set of probes, and the result is a pattern that is, generally, different for each individual, although it resembles those of their parents and blood relations.

DNA fingerprinting is used to establish paternity and in forensic work, where biological samples such as hair, semen or blood from the scene of the crime are matched with samples from suspects. The technique is not a foolproof method of establishing identity, however. First, there is more chance of two humans having similar DNA fingerprints than was previously thought – this is because the human race does not breed at random, so there is less than total mixing of genetic material. Secondly, there are technical reasons why DNA fingerprints have to be handled with caution. Any experiments involving biological materials such as restriction enzymes and DNA are very sensitive to temperature, pH and contamination. If an enzyme is stored at the wrong temperature, for example, it will not give reliable results. Tests carried out in the last few years have shown that the same sample could give different DNA fingerprints under different laboratory conditions. Scientists are now trying to set some common standards for the technique.

## Gene therapy – the ultimate cure for genetic disease?

Genetic engineering can be carried out on humans by transfecting a human cell line with a **retrovirus** (RNA virus) vector containing the gene to be inserted and then injecting the cells into a human subject.

Clinical trials of human gene therapy are already under way in patients suffering from two inherited diseases. The first trial aims to correct a rare disease of the immune system caused by the lack of an enzyme known as **adenosine deaminase** (ADA). The patients were injected with lymphocytes containing a normal ADA gene. The gene therapy has resulted in a significantly improved immune function in the patients treated. The second trial involved patients suffering from familial hypercholesterolaemia. These patients lack LDL receptors, and were treated with liver cells containing a normal LDL gene. No results are yet available, but similar experiments on rabbits showed a reduction of 30 per cent in circulating cholesterol levels. Transgenic animals with defective human genes play an important part in gene therapy research, as medical models of the disease.

Many of the existing single inherited gene defects, such as haemophilia and cystic fibrosis, are targets for gene therapy, as are genetic diseases acquired during a person's lifetime, such as cancer. But it is likely that, at least for the foreseeable future, medical researchers will have to confine their work to somatic gene therapy. Using germ cells for gene therapy would mean that the new genes would be inherited by the offspring of the people who had been treated. While this would eradicate the disease from the family, avoiding any further treatment, both the medical profession and the general public have doubts about the wisdom of manipulating the human gene pool in this way.

### 8.5   Genetic engineering: the problems

Many people worry about tampering with genes. We have the power to create new life-forms with genetic engineering, but we do not know what the hidden costs of interfering with evolution might be. So far, no harm seems to have come from releasing **genetically manipulated organisms** (GMOs) into the environment. These have been mainly microbes designed to protect plants from disease and frost damage. GMOs have marker genes engineered into their genome so their spread can be easily tracked.

GMOs used in the laboratory are usually weakened by engineering special nutritional requirements into the genes so that they could not survive outside. For instance, you could mutate a gene for an enzyme needed for amino acid synthesis so that the GMO would have a special requirement for this amino acid, and would not survive under normal conditions. The retroviruses used in gene therapy have the genes that make them virulent removed before being used in an experiment.

But however safe GMOs turn out to be, there are still difficult ethical problems to be faced. The products of genetic engineering are new life-forms, but no one is really sure whether they can or should be patented. The first patented life-form was the 'oncomouse' produced at Harvard University. This animals contains genes that make it susceptible to cancer. It is a useful model for the study of human cancer. Patenting the Harvard mouse has caused a storm of controversy and confusion in Europe, which is causing investors to hold back from biotechnology. The attempt by some US scientists to patent human genes – the result of their work on the Human Genome Project – has led to similar difficulties. Many people say that the whole issue of patenting gives genetic engineering a poor public image and undermines human dignity.

There is also the issue of 'gene plunder' to be considered. Once the genes of useful plants are taken from developing countries, these could be (and have been) cloned into cells and the products made in Western countries. This could damage income from cash crops, such as coffee, in the countries where these plants originated.

**QUESTION**   **7 You want to set up a company to produce blue roses and frost-resistant strawberries by genetic engineering. Outline a process by which you think you could do this. Include the advantages and disadvantages of your plan. List all the obstacles you will have to overcome and how you would try to do this. Suppose your project is successful. What other products would you try to develop, using the same technique?**

## Summary of Chapter 8

1   Genetic engineering involves the transfer of genes from one species to another, using restriction and ligation enzymes to insert the gene into a vector that carries the DNA into a host cell, where it multiplies.

2   Many human proteins have been produced by genetic engineering of microbial or mammalian cells.

3   Transgenic plants are produced by using a bacterial vector or by inserting DNA directly into plant cells.

4   Transgenic plants can be resistant to insect attack, or to herbicide application. They may also make useful products.

5   Transgenic animals produce human proteins in their milk and serve as models of human disease.

6   DNA probes can be used to diagnose genetic disease or to establish identity. They work by base-pairing with the gene of interest and are labelled for easy detection.

7   Genetic engineering creates new life-forms and raises questions about patenting and interfering with the process of evolution.

# Examination questions

1   Discuss the implications of genetic engineering, with reference to specific examples. (London, S)
2   New developments present new opportunities to alter the genetic make-up of domestic animals, plants and people. Describe the various ways in which these organisms can be genetically manipulated and discuss the advantages and disadvantages of such manipulation. (JMB, now NEAB, S)

### Human Insulin Production

**Figure 8.4**

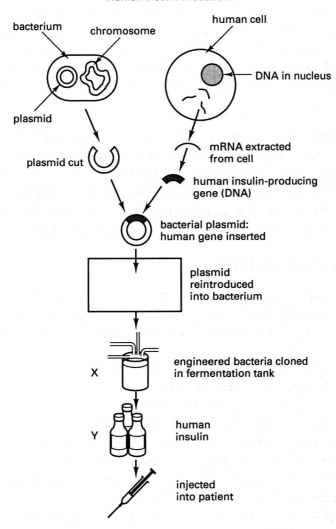

3   Figure 8.4 shows the stages involved in the synthesis of insulin by
    genetically engineered bacteria.
    (a)   (i) What is a 'plasmid'?
          (ii) Describe how the bacterial plasmid is cut prior to the
              insertion of the human insulin-producing gene.
          (iii) Draw the bacterium with its reintroduced plasmid which
              should appear in the box on the diagram.
    (b) The human insulin-producing gene is isolated from messager
        RNA molecules.
          (i) Suggest why mRNA is used rather than DNA.
          (ii) Name a cell which would be a suitable source of the
              mRNA.
    (c)   (i) What it meant by the term 'gene cloning'?
          (ii) Explain the purpose of cloning the bacteria at stage X.
    (d) Suggest two processes which must occur between stages X
        and Y.
    (e) In the past, the only available insulin for diabetics has been
        that extracted from cows or pigs. Suggest three advantages
        that genetically engineered insulin could have compared with
        beef or pork insulin. (WJEC)
4   Suggest how genetic engineering could be important in the
    treatment of disease. (London, part of question)
5   Discuss the advantages and disadvantages of genetic engineering
    compared with traditional industrial techniques of drug
    production. (London, A/S)
6   (a) Explain the theoretical basis of genetic fingerprinting.
    (b) Describe the practical procedures involved in making a
        genetic fingerprint.
    (c) How can this technique be useful in forensic science?
        (UCLES)

# chapter 9

# Enzymes

None of the chemical activities of the cell would be possible without enzymes. Enzymes are globular proteins that catalyse specific biochemical reactions. All chemical reactions have an **activation energy**, $E_a$, as shown in Figure 9.1. This is the energy required to orient the reactants into an arrangement called the transition state – an intermediate stage through which they must pass to form the products of the reaction. Enzymes work by lowering this activation energy, and have the effect of speeding up biochemical reactions, some of which could otherwise take hundreds of years to occur to any significant extent.

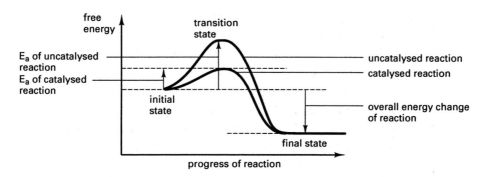

Figure 9.1 Energy diagram showing a catalysed and uncatalysed chemical reaction.

## 9.1 Enzymes are specific

The high specificity of enzymes contributes greatly to the organisation of cellular activity. Enzymes are specific in two ways: each acts on a specific type of substrate, and each catalyses either a single chemical reaction or a group of closely related reactions. You can often tell which kind of reaction an enzyme catalyses from its name. **Proteases** (or proteinases) break down proteins, while **oxidases** and **hydrolases** catalyse oxidation and hydrolysis respectively.

QUESTION

1 **What is the function of (a) a lipase, (b) a polymerase, (c) a reductase and (d) a ligase? Give examples of each.**

Substrate specificity is demonstrated by the protease family. Trypsin cleaves only at basic amino acids such as lysine and arginine, while chymotrypsin cleaves at amino acids phenylalanine, tyrosine and tryptophan.

Thrombin, which plays a key role in blood clotting, cleaves only the Arg–Gly bond of the protein fibrinogen. All these cleave at the carboxy rather than the amino side of the residue.

QUESTION   2 **Part of the amino acid sequence of the protein fibrinogen is shown below:**
**Val-Asn-Asp-Asn-Glu-Glu-Gly-Phe-Phe-Ser-Ala-Arg-Gly-His-Arg-Pro-Leu-Asp-Lys-Lys**
**Mark where (a) trypsin, (b) chymotrypsin and (c) thrombin would cleave the sequence.**

Enzymes are specific because of the way in which they bind to their substrate. The original theory of how the enzyme interacts with its substrate came from the German chemist Emil Fischer in the late nineteenth century. Fischer suggested that enzymes have an **active site** – a specific region of the molecule that binds the substrate.

X-ray analysis and computer models of enzyme tertiary structures have confirmed the active site theory. The active site is often a crevice or cleft inside the molecule that fits the substrate. This led Fischer to compare the substrate – active site interaction to a lock and a key (Figure 9.2). The active site theory was modified by Daniel Koshland in 1959. He suggested a more dynamic picture of enzyme action, which he called the **induced fit hypothesis** (Figure 9.2). Substrate binding modifies the shape of the active site. Rather than a lock and a key, the substrate – active site complex is like a hand fitting into a glove.

**Figure 9.2 Lock and key and induced fit models of enzyme– substrate binding.**

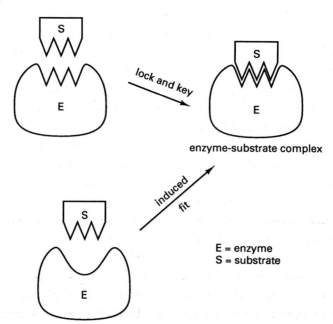

enzyme-substrate complex

E = enzyme
S = substrate

The active site only accounts for a small part of the whole enzyme molecule, with generally three or four amino acids playing a crucial role. It is important to realise that these amino acids are not usually next to each other in the sequence of the enzyme. It is the folding of the protein into its tertiary structure that brings them close together.

**3 Explain how a mutation at an active site residue could alter an enzyme's activity.**   QUESTION

Many enzymes require the presence of **cofactors** for their activity. These are non-protein molecules. They could be metal ions such as calcium, which is needed for the functioning of blood-clotting enzymes, or small organic molecules. These are either prosthetic groups, such as haem, or coenzymes such as NAD and NADP.

**4 How do haem and NAD function as a cofactors?**   QUESTION

### 9.2   Some substances inhibit enzyme action

Although enzymes are specific, the active site can bind substances other than the substrate. These substances are called **inhibitors**. They block the action of the enzyme by occupying the active site so that the substrate–enzyme complex cannot form. Inhibitors of this type fall into two groups – irreversible and reversible.

**Irreversible enzyme inhibitors** bind very tightly to the active site, completely blocking its activity. Examples include diisopropylfluorophosphate (DFP), which locks on to active site serine residues in proteases and esterases. DFP inhibits the enzyme acetylcholinesterase, which breaks down the neurotransmitter acetylcholine. Acetylcholine is a chemical messenger that passes nerve impulses from one nerve cell to another. If it is not broken down by acetylcholinesterase, nerve impulses are transmitted in an uncontrolled way, leading to extended muscle contraction, paralysis and death. Acetylcholinesterase inhibitors, such as DFP, have been used as nerve gases in human chemical warfare. They are also the basis of some insecticides, such as parathion.

Cysteine residues in enzymes are particularly vulnerable to irreversible inhibition. This is how heavy metals such as mercury and arsenic, and compounds such as iodoacetic acid, exert their toxic effects.

**Reversible enzyme inhibitors** bind more weakly to the active site than irreversible inhibitors do and can be displaced by the substrate, if high enough concentrations are present. Reversible inhibition can be useful in the design of drugs and was the basis of the first antibiotics. During the Second World War, sulphonamides were widely used to combat microbial infections among troops. The sulphonamides resemble a substance called *para*-aminobenzoate

(PAB), which is essential to the growth of some pathogenic bacteria. PAB is used in the synthesis of folic acid, an important cofactor. In the presence of sulphonamide, PAB cannot bind to the enzyme that transforms it into folic acid. Deprived of folic acid, the bacteria die. Such reversible inhibitors, which compete for the active site with the enzyme's substrate, are called **competitive inhibitors** (Figure 9.3).

Figure 9.3 (a)
Competitive
and (b)
non-
competitive
enzyme
inhibition.

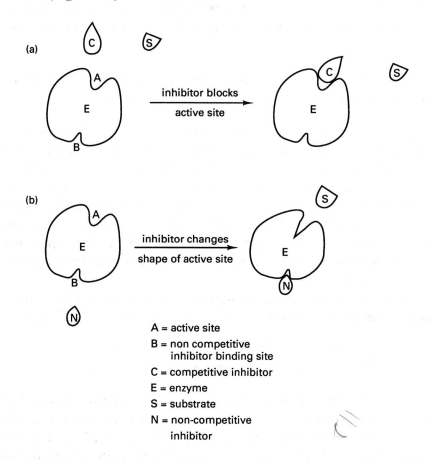

(a)

inhibitor blocks
active site

(b)

inhibitor changes
shape of active site

A = active site
B = non competitive
      inhibitor binding site
C = competitive inhibitor
E = enzyme
S = substrate
N = non-competitive
      inhibitor

The final category of inhibitors do not bind with the active site at all. Since proteins are flexible molecules, binding of a substance at one site can alter the shape of the rest of the molecule. This is sometimes known as the allosteric effect. **Non-competitive** or **allosteric inhibitors** work by altering the shape of the active site so that it no longer binds the substrate (Figure 9.3). An important example of this is the inhibition of a key enzyme in glycolysis, phosphofructokinase, by ATP. When the ATP levels in the cell are high, there is less need for glycolysis. Inhibition of the enzyme by its eventual product, ATP, is a powerful method of control of enzyme activity.

## 9.3    Enzyme activity depends upon reaction conditions

Like all proteins, enzymes are denatured by extremes of pH. Most enzymes work best in the pH range 6.0–8.0, because this maintains the charges on acidic and basic residue side chains, which could be crucial in maintaining the enzyme's tertiary structure (Figure 9.4a). Outside this pH range, the enzyme could become denatured. There are exceptions, such as pepsin with its pH maximum of 2.

QUESTION

**5 From its pH maximum, what type of amino acids would you expect to find at the active site of pepsin? Sketch its pH profile.**

Similarly, enzymes are denatured at high temperatures. However, the rate of all chemical reactions, including enzyme reactions, approximately doubles for every 10°C temperature rise, which means that there are two opposing trends to consider in evaluating the effect of temperature on enzyme action (Figure 9.4b). Some enzymes have been extracted from organisms that live at very high temperatures. For example, Taq polymerase, from *Thermophilus aquaticus*, which lives in hot springs, is useful in the PCR reaction, which requires heating to about 70°C. Proteases that are active at high temperatures are useful in detergents.

The effect of temperature on enzyme activity is measured by a quantity called the **temperature coefficient**, $Q_{10}$, which is given by the following ratio:

$$Q_{10} = \frac{\text{rate of reaction at } (x+10)°\text{C}}{\text{rate of reaction at } x°\text{C}}$$

The study of how enzyme activity varies with substrate concentration is known as **enzyme kinetics**. For many enzymes, the rate of reaction increases with substrate concentration up to a limit (Figure 9.4c). The limit occurs because of saturation of enzyme sites – being a catalyst, the enzyme is usually present in far smaller quantities than the substrate.

The plateau occurs when every active site in the enzyme is occupied, or saturated, with substrate. The enzyme concentration becomes rate-limiting under these conditions.

QUESTION

**6 How could you increase the rate of enzyme action in Figure 9.4c?**

### The Michaelis–Menten model of enzyme action

Data from enzyme kinetic studies led Leonor Michaelis and Maud Menten to propose the following equation for enzyme action:

$$E + S \rightleftharpoons ES \rightarrow P$$

**Figure 9.4 The effect of reaction conditions on enzyme activity. (a) Activity–pH curve for an enzyme. (b) The effect of temperature on the activity of an enzyme such as salivary amylase. (c) Effect of substrate concentration on the rate of an enzyme-controlled reaction.**

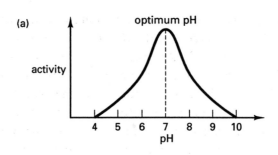

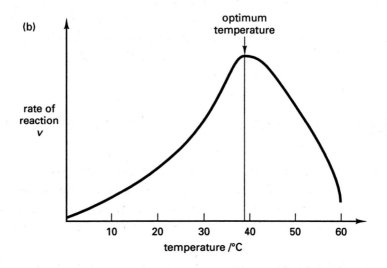

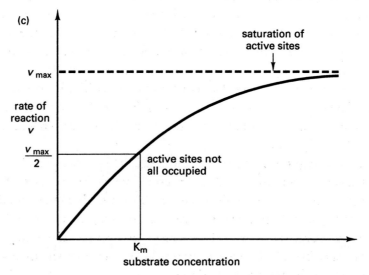

The enzyme (E) and substrate (S) form a complex, ES, which then forms the products P. Two important quantities emerge from the Michaelis–Menten model: $V_{max}$ is the maximum rate of enzyme activity for a given enzyme concentration; $K_m$ is the substrate concentration for which the rate of reaction is half of $V_{max}$. This is a measure of the affinity of the enzyme for its substrate. Low values denote a high affinity. Enzymes show a very wide range of $K_m$ values; that of lysozyme is $6\,\mu M$, while that of chymotrypsin is $5000\,\mu M$. Although the $K_m$ value is characteristic of an enzyme, it also depends on substrate, pH, temperature and the nature of its medium.

Another important property of an enzyme is its **turnover number** – the number of substrate molecules turned into products per unit time (when the enzyme is saturated with substrate). Again, this value varies widely between enzymes. The one with the fastest turnover number (600 000 molecules per second) is carbonic anhydrase, which catalyses the dissolving of carbon dioxide in plasma prior to its elimination via the lungs.

## 9.4    Enzymes can be exploited for human needs

The world market for enzymes is worth hundreds of millions of pounds. The largest use is in the manufacture of detergents and in the food industry. There are also increasing applications of enzymes in the fields of medical research, diagnosis and treatment. Table 9.1 gives a breakdown of the world enzyme market.

These enzymes are produced mainly from microbial sources. To meet demand, high-yielding strains are used. But some enzymes are not produced by microbes and are extracted instead from animals and plants. For example, trypsin, lipases and rennet are often extracted from animal sources. Plant enzymes, such as amylases, papain and bromelain, are preferred by the food industry because there is no risk of contamination with endotoxins (substances produced by bacteria that can cause disease). In fact, the industrial enzymes are nearly all produced from only 25 of the thousands of known microbial species – this is for safety reasons.

The advantages of using enzymes in industrial processes include the mild conditions of temperature and pressure under which they operate, which saves on energy costs, and their high specificity, which leads to pure products that require little processing. For this reason, there is a growing interest in using enzymes in industrial chemical processes other than those in Table 9.1. Disadvantages include the expense of producing enzymes and their sensitivity to denaturation by their surroundings.

These drawbacks can often be overcome by enzyme **immobilisation**. This involves chemically linking the enzyme to a solid support, usually some form of polymer, or trapping it inside beads of a gel. Both these techniques mean that the enzyme can be re-used, because it does not dissolve in its immobilised

**Table 9.1   The uses of enzymes**

| Enzyme type | Use |
| --- | --- |
| *Industrial (90 per cent of total)* | |
| Proteases (60 per cent) | detergents, cheese making |
| Carbohydratases (25 per cent) | bread making |
| Lipases (10 per cent) | detergents |
| Glucose isomerase (5 per cent) | production of high-fructose syrup |
| | |
| *Medical, analytical, research (10 per cent)* | |
| Restriction enzymes | genetic research and diagnosis |
| Proteases | anti-thrombolytic therapy |
| Various | biosensors, antibiotic production |

form and does not get washed away at the end of the reaction. Immobilisation also offers the enzyme some protection against denaturation.

Immobilised enzymes used in industry include glucose isomerase, which is used in the production of high-fructose syrup (see Chapter 5), and penicillin acylase for the manufacture of penicillin-like antibiotics.

**QUESTION   7 How could immobilisation decrease the activity of an enzyme?**

  **The largest use of industrial enzymes is in detergents**

**'Biological'** detergents are those which contain enzymes. Protein stains such as blood and egg are hard to remove from fabric by normal washing because they denature when the stain dries or in a hot wash. Once denatured, they become less soluble in water and more difficult to remove. The first biological washing powders contained proteases such as Alcalase™, which is stable at the alkaline pH of the detergent. Alcalase operates best at a temperature of around 60°C, taking between 15 and 30 minutes to break down most protein stains into soluble fragments that are easily washed away. The modern trend towards cooler washing temperatures has led to the development of an alternative protease, Savinase™, which works best around 50°C.

Proteases have no effect on starchy or fatty stains, however. In recent years, amylases have been added to biological detergents to get rid of starch-based stains such as spaghetti, sauces and baby food. Lipases have also been added to get rid of greasy stains.

The most advanced detergents condition the fabric, as well as removing stains. Washing damages cotton fibres, breaking down the long cellulose polymers into microfibrils, which give the surface of the material a fuzzy appearance. Detergent cellulases remove these, improving and softening the texture. It also aids cleaning by removing the dirt that tends to cling to the microfibrils.

**8 Which types of fabric should never be soaked in biological detergents and why? Why do enzymes only make up about 1 per cent by mass of most biological washing powders?**    QUESTION

## 9.6    Enzymes work in the food industry

Cheese, bread, wine and fruit juice are among the products that receive enzymatic treatment during their production. Cheese is made from milk by two main enzymatic processes. Lactic acid is first produced from lactose by bacterial action, which lowers the pH of the milk. Addition of the protease chymosin then partly breaks down casein proteins, forming a solid mass known as the curd. As the curd matures, further action by chymosin, and bacterial and milk enzymes leads to a variety of flavours and aromas.

Chymosin occurs in rennet, an extract from calf stomach. A genetically engineered chymosin is now available that is produced by cloning the calf chymosin gene in the fungus *Kluyveromyces lactis*. This is used to manufacture a range of vegetarian cheeses.

**Pectin** is one of the most abundant carbohydrates on Earth. It holds the cells of fruits together by acting as a kind of glue. As fruit ripens, the pectin partly solubilises. This produces gels when the juice is extracted from the fruit. Pectinases are essential for breaking down this pectin in the processing of fruit to make juice. The extent of pectinase treatment needed depends upon the fruit and the type of juice required. Once orange juice has been extracted, for example, the residual pectinases are removed by pasteurisation so that the pectin-containing particles that give it its cloudiness are retained. To obtain a clear juice, more pectinase is added, which has the effect of precipitating out these particles so that a clear juice can be filtered off.

Other enzymes are used in the manufacture of fruit juices. Naringin is a bitter-tasting substance present in citrus fruits. This can be removed by naringinase, an enzyme extracted from the fungus *Aspergillus*. Cellulases added with pectinases aid the extraction of pigments from the skin of the fruit by breaking down the cell walls. This is particularly important in making juices from blackcurrants and grapes.

**9 Papain, a protease from the papaya fruit, is used as a meat tenderiser. How does it work?**    QUESTION

## 9.7    Analytical uses of enzymes rely on their specificity

Biological fluids such as blood are a complex mixture, and analysis of a specific substance such as glucose requires techniques that are specific, accurate and sensitive. Enzymes are the basis for many new tests for biochemically active compounds.

One of these, the enzyme-linked immunosorbent assay (ELISA), can detect tiny amounts ($10^{-8}$ g cm$^{-3}$) of proteins in biological fluids such as serum. ELISA relies on the use of antibodies as well as proteins. Figure 9.5 shows how ELISA works. The procedure is carried out on a plastic plate, which contains a number of small wells. First, a small amount of buffer containing an antibody that is known to bind to the protein (X) under test is loaded into the wells. The antibody molecules bind to the surface of the wells. Then the test serum or other fluid is added, along with controls. Protein X will bind to the antibody, whereas other proteins in the test fluid can be washed away. Then a second antibody that can bind X is added (a protein has many sites on its surface for binding different antibodies). The second antibody has already been linked to an enzyme. By this stage, every molecule of the test protein is linked to an enzyme tag. The enzyme is chosen so that it produces an easily detectable product from a substrate. The final step is the addition of this substrate. Now every well containing the test protein can be identified, within the sensitivity limit of the method. A favourite enzyme to use in ELISA is **peroxidase**, which gives a bright yellow colour with hydrogen peroxide in the presence of a substance called *ortho*-phenylenediamine (OPD).

ELISA is widely used in the diagnosis of infectious diseases, where it can detect antigens and antibodies from a wide range of viruses, bacteria and parasites. It can also be used to monitor hormone levels (for example, in pregnancy testing) and in food quality control. Adulteration of beef with horse meat, pig meat or even ground-up soybean can be detected by ELISA on the basis of the foreign protein in the sample of meat.

**Figure 9.5**

**Enzyme-linked immunosorbent assay.**

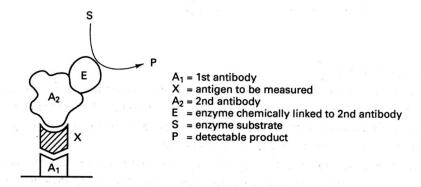

A$_1$ = 1st antibody
X  = antigen to be measured
A$_2$ = 2nd antibody
E  = enzyme chemically linked to 2nd antibody
S  = enzyme substrate
P  = detectable product

Biosensors are devices that use an electrical transducer to turn a biochemical signal from an enzyme into an electrical output. For example, glucose oxidase can be used as the basis for a biosensor to detect the amount of glucose in blood (Figure 9.6). The enzyme catalyses the reaction between oxygen and glucose to give gluconic acid. The oxygen consumption in the blood sample is measured by a transducer called an oxygen electrode. This gives a measure of the glucose level, because the higher this is, the more oxygen is consumed. Although biosensor technology is still in its early stages, potential and developing applications include routine clinical testing and detection of toxins in food and water. The aim is to construct instruments that are robust, easy to use and sensitive.

Many new diagnostic test strips that include enzymes have been developed in the last decade to take clinical testing out of the hospital and into the doctor's surgery or the home. For instance, glucose in urine can be measured by a test strip with glucose oxidase and peroxidase immobilised on a cellulose pad. After dipping it into the sample, the pad changes colour and can be read off against a colour test chart. Many clinical tests can be loaded onto a single strip or a multi-layered slide.

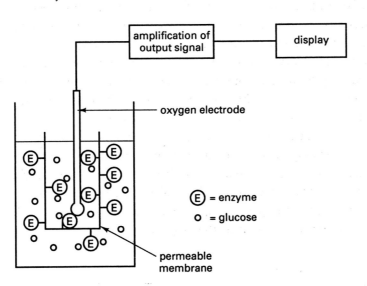

Figure 9.6

Inside a glucose biosensor.

## The clotbusters

When an animal is injured, excessive blood loss is prevented by the formation of a **fibrin** clot at the site of the wound. Fibrin is a polymer that is formed by the action of **thrombin**, a protease, on **fibrinogen**. The fibrin clot is eventually dissolved by another protease, called **plasmin**.

The **coagulation** process that leads to fibrin clot formation is a complicated one, which involves several proteins other than thrombin. Problems arise when the coagulation system does not work properly. Either there is excessive bleeding, as in haemophilia, or clots form in the wrong places, such as the coronary arteries and the blood vessel leading to the brain. Such blockages of vital blood vessels are known as **thromboses** and are a major cause of death because they lead to heart attack or stroke.

The aim of thrombolytic therapy is to activate plasmin so that these dangerous clots can be dissolved (Figure 9.7). Three enzymes are currently used for this purpose – **urokinase, streptokinase** and **tissue plasminogen activator** (tPA). All three are proteases, which activate plasminogen to form plasmin. Streptokinase is isolated from bacteria, and can cause adverse immunological reactions. It is also not very specific and can cause bleeding problems. Urokinase comes from urine, but is expensive to isolate. tPA has been made by genetic engineering; it is more expensive, but not more effective than streptokinase.

**Figure 9.7 The role of thrombolytic proteins in dissolving blood clots.**

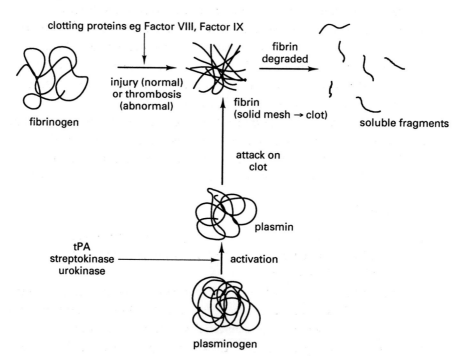

For this reason, attempts are being made to engineer the tPA molecule to make it more effective. These protein engineering strategies usually involve making deliberate mutations into genes before cloning them into host cells, a process known as **site-directed mutagenesis**. These strategies can reveal a great deal about a protein's function.

Genetic engineers trying to redesign tPA have three aims: to increase the lifetime of tPA in the body, to increase its affinity to fibrin, and to decrease its interaction with its inhibitors.

**10** Sketch graphs showing the variation of enzyme activity with substrate    QUESTION
concentration for tPA and an engineered tPA with greater affinity for
fibrin.

## Summary of Chapter 9

**1**   Enzymes are biological catalysts that work by lowering the
activation energy of chemical reactions in the cell.

**2**   Enzymes are specific for substrate and reaction type. The
substrate is bound to an active site within the protein to form an
enzyme–substrate complex.

**3**   Enzymes can be inhibited. Inhibitors fall into three classes:
irreversible, reversible and allosteric.

**4**   The rate of enzyme activity depends upon substrate
concentration. When all the active sites on an enzyme are
saturated, the enzyme concentration becomes rate-limiting.

**5**   Enzyme activity is affected by temperature and pH. The rate of
activity increases with temperature, but denaturation of the
protein begins above $40\,^{\circ}C$, leading to a temperatue maximum,
beyond which activity falls. pH changes can denature enzymes or
alter the charge on residues at the active site.

**6**   Enzymes are used in industry in detergents and in food processing.

**7**   Analytical methods based on enzymes include ELISA and
biosensors – these techniques are very sensitive and are used
extensively in clinical diagnosis.

## Examination questions

**1**   (a) Explain why the rate of an enzyme-catalysed reaction is
affected by changes to (i) pH, (ii) temperature and
(iii) enzyme concentration.

(b) For each of the following give a named example of an enzyme
which is (i) found in solution in a cell, (ii) fixed on membranes
and (iii) secreted into external substrates. (London)

**2**   Read the passage, and then answer the questions which follow.
   'Collagen is a fibrous protein, found in many human tissues,
including cartilage. Collagen fibres are constantly being broken
down and reformed. The fibres are broken down by enzymes
called collagenases, which are produced by cells in the cartilage.
Collagenase is a powerful enzyme; just 1 mg of collagenase can
break down 3 g of collagen in one hour at body temperature.
   People with arthritis produce large amounts of collagenase.
This leads to progressive destruction of cartilage, resulting in
very painful joints.

Such powerful enzymes need careful control. Cells in cartilage also produce an inhibitor of collagenase which can prevent the breakdown of collagen. Pharmaceutical companies are now using knowledge of the shape and properties of collagenase to produce artificial inhibitors which may one day be used as drugs to help sufferers from arthritis.'

(a) Describe how you would expect the tertiary structure of collagen to differ from that of collagenase.

(b) Explain how it is possible that 'just 1 mg of collagenase can break down 3 g of collagen in one hour at body temperature'.

(c) Explain two ways in which the inhibitor produced by the cells in cartilage may prevent the breaking down of collagen. Explain your answer fully.

(d) Suggest why pharmaceutical companies are using knowledge of the shape and properties of collagenase, rather than the natural inhibitor, to produce artificial inhibitors. (UCLES)

3. Discuss the role of enzymes in cell metabolism, and comment on those factors which affect enzyme activity. (London)

4. (a) What is a biosensor?

(b) Explain how a biosensor might be used to regulate insulin release in a person with diabetes. (UCLES)

## appendix ⊳ Some basic chemistry

### Atoms and molecules

All matter is made up of tiny particles known as **atoms**. An **element** contains only one kind of atom and there are 92 naturally occurring elements

Atoms themselves are made up of smaller particles. There is a central **nucleus** containing two kinds of particle, the **neutron** and the **proton**. The latter has a positive electrical charge, which is balanced by an equal number of negatively charged **electrons** found outside the nucleus. Most of the atom's mass resides in the nucleus (the mass of an electron is only about 1/2000 that of the proton). Atoms of different elements have different numbers of protons. For instance, a carbon atom has six protons, while a uranium atom has 92. The proton number of an element is called its **atomic number**, while the number of protons and neutrons added together is known as its **mass number.**

Atoms of the same element may have different numbers of neutrons. These different forms of the element are **isotopes**. Some isotopes are **radioactive**. Their nuclei emit radiation, which can be detected by a counter. In experiments this enables us to track an individual atom in a chemical reaction – the technique is often called **radio-labelling**. Experiments using $^{14}$C, an isotope of carbon, have been used to explore the chemistry of photosynthesis (see Chapter 6).

Atoms usually go round in groups, known as **molecules** (although inert gases such as helium consist of individual atoms, as do pure metals). The atoms in a molecule may be the same, as in hydrogen, $H_2$. More commonly, the atoms in a molecule will differ from each other. Molecules of methane, for example, consist of one carbon atom and four hydrogen atoms.

Substances made up of only one kind of molecule are known as **compounds**. Substances that contain more than one compound are mixtures (air is a mixture).

Chemistry uses a short-hand based upon symbols for the elements and formulae for compounds that show which, and how many, atoms their molecules contain. When two or more compounds react together chemically to produce new compounds, the change is represented by a chemical equation, which uses this short-hand. For example, when methane burns in oxygen (or air), carbon dioxide and water are produced. This can be represented by:

$$CH_4 + 2O_2 \rightarrow CO_2 + 2H_2O$$

Notice that the number of atoms (of each element) on the left-hand side is equal to the number on the right-hand side.

Molecules come in a range of sizes. They can be put on a size scale that compares their mass with that of a standard atomic mass unit (remembering that the atom is the fundamental unit of matter). This gives the **relative**

**molecular mass** ($M_r$) of the molecule. As $M_r$ is a ratio, it has no units. Some of the molecules that are important in biochemistry, such as proteins, have very high relative molecular masses because they are very large molecules containing thousands of atoms.

Many biological molecules are **polymers**. These are long chains of simple repeating units. An example of a simple polymer that is in common use would be polythene, which consists of thousands of ethene ($C_2H_4$) molecules linked together in a chain. Biological polymers include proteins, DNA and cellulose.

Specific groups of atoms within a molecule can be important in contributing to the overall properties of a substance. For example, sugars contain hydroxyl (OH) groups, which make them soluble in water.

## Bonding

It is the electrons that join atoms together in compounds. Either one or more electrons are transferred between atoms to give an **ionic bond**, or they are shared to give **covalent bonds**. Most important biological molecules are carbon (or organic) compounds, and these are usually covalently bonded. Sometimes chemical formulae are written in a form that displays the bonds, which are usually shown as a single line (there are examples throughout this text). In these structural formulae, carbon and hydrogen atoms themselves are often omitted, for the sake of clarity, but are understood to be present at the junction, or ends, of the bonds (see, for example, the structural formula of chlorophyll in Chapter 6).

In biochemistry, **hydrogen bonds** are particularly important. These are weak bonds that arise between a hydrogen atom bonded to nitrogen, oxygen or fluorine and a neighbouring nitrogen, oxygen or fluorine atom. For instance, hydrogen fluoride can hydrogen bond as follows:

$$H–F\cdots H–F\cdots H–F\cdots$$

where the dots represent the hydrogen bonds. Water is extensively hydrogen bonded.

## Chemical reactions

The types of chemical reaction that are important in biochemistry are the following.

1  **Oxidation** and **reduction**. Oxidation is the loss of electrons in a reaction. Reduction is the gain of electrons in a reaction. There is no oxidation without reduction. When glucose is oxidised to carbon dioxide, for example, oxygen is reduced to water. Sometimes oxidation is described as the loss of hydrogen atoms and reduction as the gain of hydrogen atoms.

2  **Condensation.** Two or more molecules join together to form a larger molecule with the loss of a small molecule (usually water).

This happens when alcohols and organic acids condense together to form an ester and water (for example, when fats, which are esters, are formed from glycerol – an alcohol – and fatty acids).

3   **Hydrolysis**. This is the reverse of condensation. It occurs when water splits a molecule up into two or more smaller molecules, such as, when sugar is split up into fructose and glucose.

## Solutions

Water is the universal solvent for biochemical reactions. Substances that are readily soluble in water are said to be **hydrophilic**. They usually contain ionic bonds, such as sodium chloride, or have one or more **polar** covalent bonds. The O–H bond of a hydroxyl group, for example, is polar because the shared electrons are pulled towards the oxygen atom. The C–C bond is non-polar because the atoms at the end of the bond are the same – there is no preferential pull of electrons to either end. The C–H bond is also non-polar. Substances with mainly **non-polar** bonds (such as lipids, which have a high hydrocarbon content) will tend to be **hydrophobic** or insoluble in water.

An important property of solutions in biological systems is **pH**, which is a measure of hydrogen ion concentration. The pH scale ranges from 0 to 14. Solutions with a pH below 7 are said to be **acidic**, while those with pH above 7 are **basic** (pH 7 denotes neutrality).

Substances that donate hydrogen ions are acids; substances that accept hydrogen ions are bases. The hydrogen ion is sometimes also called a proton, because the hydrogen atom consists of just one proton and one electron. If the electron is lost in a chemical reaction, a proton or hydrogen ion remains.

## Units

The units used in this text are SI units, which are internationally recognised as the units of science. Some of the more important ones follow:

1   Energy is measured in joules (J) or, more commonly, kilojoules (kJ).

2   Length is measured in metres, but on a molecular scale a more useful unit is the **nanometre** (nm), which is $10^{-9}$ m. The **micrometre** (μm), which is $10^{-6}$ m, is also often used.

3   In biochemistry, amounts of substance are measured in moles rather than in grams or kilograms. Concentrations are often given in moles per litre, which is abbreviated to M (so a 0.1 M solution contains 0.1 moles in one litre). The mole relates more exactly to the actual number of molecules involved in a chemical reaction than do grams or kilograms (details of how to work these out are not required for A level biology, but you should recognise the symbol M described above).

4   Volume should be measured in cm³ (not ml), where 1000 cm³ is one litre (l or dm³).

# Answers to questions in the text

## Chapter 1

1 Mercury damages the nervous system – for example, in the Minamata episode, many Japanese suffered brain damage after mercury-contaminated fish were consumed. There is also the 'Mad Hatter' in *Alice in Wonderland* (possibly a reference to the fact that mercury compounds were used in felt making, so were an occupational hazard to hatters). Other toxic elements include lead (nervous system), cadmium (kidneys), uranium and plutonium (both carcinogenic), arsenic (highly toxic to many body systems) and possibly aluminium (linked to Alzheimer's disease).

2 The Si–Si bond is too weak to allow long chains to build up – these are always hydrolysed to form the more stable silicon dioxide. Long chains are needed for information carrying (DNA, RNA) and enzyme function (protein).

3 Urey and Miller had to make certain assumptions about the nature of the early atmosphere in the absence of firm evidence. The composition of gases could be wrong. Frequency of 'lightning' is unknown. There is no simulation of meteorite impact. Other theories could be tested by including rocks for silicon template (Cairns-Smith), seeding the mixture with amino acids from 'meteorites' to see what is synthesised, and simulating a hydrothermal vent environment (no lightning, higher temperature).

4 Main problem is lack of nitrogen, phosphorus and sulphur. Winemakers add ammonium sulphate and ammonium phosphate as yeast nutrient. Fruit usually provides trace elements.

5 Weigh sample of fresh plant or animal material. Heat in oven to constant mass and work out percentage water driven off by heating. Spinach collapses on heating as water content of cells boils off. Strawberries lose their texture when ice crystals destroy cellular structure on freezing.

6 See text such as *Biological Science* by N. P. O. Green, G. W. Stout and D. J. Taylor, chapter 7.

7 The cells tend to clump together and develop into plants.

8 Flowchart should include sterilisation of vessel, medium, inoculation, growth, aeration, pH and temperature control, filtration, extraction and solvent recycling.

Yield is maximised by selecting a high-yielding strain, using correct conditions of aeration, pH, agitation and medium composition. Contamination must be eliminated by effective sterilisation. Costs are kept down by using cheap medium, e.g. wastes such as corn-steep liquor, and recycling organic solvent.

9   A is not a mutagen; B is a mutagen; C is toxic at the concentrations tested. Control would be water or buffer in place of test chemical to same volume as test chemical. Further investigations would include experiment with a lower concentration of C.

# Chapter 2

1   About 3500.

2   Failure of blood to clot, leading to severe bleeding problems. In this case, the cause is the change from Cys to Tyr in the sequence given.

3   Ala-Arg-Asp-Gly-Gly-Phe,
    Phe-Gly-Arg-Ala-Asp-Gly,
    Gly-Asp-Gly-Arg-Ala-Phe.

4   Include: PITC input, acid input, chromatography, colorimetric detection, analysis, display, data storage.

5   (a) Ala-Ala-Trp-Gly-Lys-Thr-Asn-Val-Lys.
    (b) Thr-Asn-Val-Lys-Ala-Ala-Trp-Gly-Lys.
    (c) The correct one is (b).

6   Edman degradation or end-group analysis with a set of proteases of known specificity.

7   No. They are too short and too long, respectively, for the formation of hydrogen bonds (0.3 nm).

8   Tortoiseshell is hard because it consists of sheets of α-helices held together by disulphide bonds, which are strong. The β-pleated sheets of silk are held together by weaker hydrogen bonds, which makes silk flexible.

9   The perming is likely to be ineffective in the presence of hydrogen peroxide – new disulphide bonds will be formed as the old ones are broken. But the process will be uncontrolled and unpredictable, leaving the hair brittle and damaged.

10  (a) Glu, Asp, Lys, Tyr, Arg, Ser, Thr, Cys, Asn, Gln, His.
    (b) Val, Ile, Phe, Trp, Gly, Ala, Leu, Pro, Met.

11  Amino acid sequencing gives the primary structure, X-ray crystallography the tertiary structure. You cannot deduce the tertiary structure from the primary structure, so both techniques are needed for a full description of a protein. (It would be impractical to use X-ray crystallography to obtain the primary structure as it is – overall – a time-consuming process compared to sequencing.)

## Chapter 3

1 He could have grown the S bacteria on a medium containing radioactively labelled phosphate. Then their DNA would have been labelled and detectable in the cells of the R bacteria after transformation.

2 If there are $3 \times 10^9$ bases and each is 0.34 nm long, then the human DNA molecule is $3 \times 10^9 \times 0.34$ nm or $3 \times 0.34$ m long. This is just over one metre.

3 (a) 50 per cent $^{14}$N DNA and 50 per cent $^{15}$N DNA.
(b) 12.5 per cent $^{15}$N DNA and 87.5 per cent $^{14}$N DNA.

4 The hydrogen bonds between the bases break and the two strands separate. This is called denaturation or melting and is reversible on cooling.

5 GATTTCGAGACCTCT.

6 Ten cycles gives an amplification of $2^{10}$ (1024) of the original sample. From one microgram you would get 1.024 mg.

## Chapter 4

1 (a) Stearic (soap is made from beef fat).
(b) Oleic, linoleic.

2 Eat about 30 g less fat per day. Eat roughly 60 g more carbohydrate to make up the difference.

3 A high-fat diet, common in the Western world, leads to atherosclerosis. Health education to eat less fat, routine testing of cholesterol levels, and cholesterol-lowering drugs could all cut the incidence of atherosclerosis.

4 Cholesterol is required for the biosynthesis of products that are manufactured in different organs of the body, e.g. oestrogen is produced by the ovary. It is also needed for cell membranes, which are present in every cell of the body.

5 The outer surface of the membrane is characterised by carbohydrate groups on glycoproteins or glycolipids. The LDL receptor would be on the outer surface to trap circulating LDL. There are intrinsic proteins that span the whole of the membrane, and extrinsic proteins that are embedded in one layer only. Some proteins form channels through the membrane. There are globular and fibrous proteins; some are glycoproteins.

6 The identification of the faulty protein in an inherited disease is the key to understanding the biochemical abnormality. In CF, once we know a membrane protein is involved, we can use drugs that facilitate transport of salt and water across the membrane to take over the faulty protein's function.

# Chapter 5

1  Bread contains sugars formed from starch by amylase during kneading. On heating, these break down to caramel. Water is removed from the sugar molecules as caramel is formed (a dehydration reaction) and can be seen rising as steam when toast is browned under a grill. Caramel gives toast its brown colour and its flavour. Dehydration makes the bread decrease in mass and gives the toast its crunchy texture. If toasting is carried too far, the sugars break down completely to carbon (the black coating of burnt toast) and water.

2  Sucralose is 500 times sweeter than sugar, so you would substitute 100 g of sugar with 100/500 g of sucralose, i.e. 0.2 g.

3  Cellulase degrades microfibrils – fragments of cellulose molecules that are formed by breakdown of full-sized cellulose on repeated washing. Microfibrils stick out from the surface of cotton fabrics, creating a rough fuzzy texture. Cellulase treatment breaks the microfibrils, removing dirt they have trapped, and restores the surface of the fabric to its former smoothness.

4  Measure a length (about one metre) of cotton thread and tie it to a clamp. Tie a small weight (about 10 g) to the end. Measure the length again to account for any knots you have made. Now gradually add to the load (the slotted weights used in physics experiments are suitable for this). Note whether there is any stretching and the load at which the thread breaks. The strength of cellulose comes from its long polymer chains. Pulling these means pulling against strong chemical bonds, which are not easily deformed or broken.

5  When starch reacts with amylase, the blue colour fades and is replaced by a range of purple to brown colours, which are characteristic of dextrins, so the reaction can be followed by testing samples with iodine at increasing time intervals. Alternatively, as glucose is produced, the reaction with Fehling's or Benedict's solution can be used to test for its presence. The mass of Cu(I) precipitate produced is a measure of the amount of glucose present.

# Chapter 6

1  Overall shape like Figure 6.1. The rate of the dark reaction depends on the carbon dioxide concentration, so there is an initial increase of rate as carbon dioxide level increases. This levels off, and light then becomes the limiting factor. This behaviour occurs because photosynthesis is a two-stage process and the separate factors influencing these stages both determine the overall rate.

2  Chlorophyll has a long hydrocarbon tail that is readily soluble in the lipid bilayer of the thylakoid membrane. The ring points inwards to the stroma.

3  Carotenoids absorb blue light (400–500 nm), so they will appear orange-red.

4  You could use radio-labelled carbon dioxide in photosynthesis experiments. The heavy oxygen would be found in the glucose.

5  Oxidising (it accepts hydrogen atoms).

6  He created his own pH gradient – in photosynthesis it is created by the action of sunlight on chlorophyll.

7  Use a fermenter to grow *Halobacterium halobium* in a saline medium.

8  Place the cells in water. They will burst, leaving the membranes behind.

9  The porphyrin ring should be retained as this part of the molecule traps the energy of sunlight.

10 They are portable, small, and have no polluting by-products. But their efficiency is very low and some may not be very sensitive to low sunlight intensities, which are the norm in many northern countries.

11 Photolysis of water was shown to be source of oxygen, G3P identified as a key intermediate in the dark stage.

12 The conversion of glucose into G3P uses up two molecules of ATP. Two are then released in the conversion of G3P into pyruvate, for each molecule of G3P. But one glucose molecule effectively creates two of G3P, so four molecules of ATP are produced in this second stage. On balance, then, in glycolysis four molecules of ATP are created and two used up. The net gain of ATP per molecule of glucose is two molecules.

13 Two molecules of ATP are produced in the TCA cycle per molecule of glucose entering glycolysis. Eight molecules of reduced hydrogen carriers are produced (remember to multiply the yield from acetyl CoA by 2 to get the numbers for glucose).

14 Twelve molecules of reduced coenzymes enter the electron transport chain for each molecule of glucose broken down.

15 The electron transport chain cannot function in the absence of oxygen, which is the terminal electron acceptor.

16 Both use energy to generate a proton gradient from reduced coenzymes. The proton gradient is linked to ATP production. Both use enzymes embedded in membranes to generate a proton gradient.

17 Reduced hydrogen carriers (reducing agents) pass electrons to a chain of hydrogen carrier proteins, releasing chemical energy as

they do so. This chemical energy is used to pump protons into the fluid-filled space of the mitochondria. This proton gradient is a store of chemical potential energy, which is released as the protons flow back into the mitochondrial matrix through channels in the enzyme ATP synthase. This proton flow activates the enzyme and generates ATP, so that the energy of the proton gradient is transformed into the chemical energy of ATP.

18 Fructose comes from the breakdown of sucrose, and occurs in honey and fruit. Galactose comes from the breakdown of lactose in milk.

19 Bacteria such as *Lactobacillus* have digested the lactose in cheese and yoghurt already, so these products are digestible by people with lactose deficiency.

# Chapter 7

1 Met-Lys-Ala-Asn-Ala-Lys-Thr-Ile-Ile-Ala.

2 (a) $4^2 = 16$, insufficient to specify 20 amino acids.
  (b) $4^4 = 256$, far more than required.

3 Make an AAAA... polynucleotide and incubate with lysine (no other amino acids), and other substances involved in protein synthesis. The product should be polylysine, i.e. a polypeptide chain containing only lysine residues. The product could be identified by amino acid analysis.

4 The haploid vegetative stage means there is no masking of recessive genes. Mutations could be detected immediately. The fungus has a short life-cycle and is easy to grow.

5 AUCGGGAUACGU.

6 CACGUACUGACG.

7 (a) AAA, AAG.
  (b) UUU, UUC.
  (c) CUU, CUC.

8 (a) Insertion.
  (b) Point.
  (c) Deletion.

9 (a) AAA to AAG.
  (b) AAA to AAT(U).
  (c) AAA to T(U)AA.

10 The regulatory gene is mutated and is not producing the repressor protein. The β-galactosidase gene is mutated in the second mutant.

11 CF – CFTR protein; SCA – haemoglobin; PKU – phenylalanine hydroxylase; osteogenesis imperfecta – collagen; familial hypercholesterolaemia – LDL receptor; muscular dystrophy – dystrophin; haemophilia – Factor VIII or Factor IX.

**12**  100 000 genes is 100 000 000 bp or $10^8$ bp. If there are $3 \times 10^9$ bp in the human genome, then $10^8/(3 \times 10^9)$ or 3 per cent codes for protein.

**13**  Sequence (a) codes for protein, (b) has a stop codon at codon 2.

# Chapter 8

**1**  (a) EcoRI produces a 'staggered cut'. The bases between the two points where the enzyme cuts (restriction sites) form two 'sticky ends', which are single-stranded. They have the sequence AATT (top strand) and TTAA (bottom strand).

   (b) HaeIII makes a straight cut, leaving 'blunt ends'. One fragment has the sequence GG (top strand) paired with CC, the other has the sequence CC (top) paired with GG.

**2**  Human insulin is a replacement for pork insulin. You cannot create human insulin from pork insulin.

   There is no such organism as 'yeast bacteria' – an organism cannot be both a yeast and a bacterium.

   Enzymes are used in genetic engineering; they are not an alternative to it.

   Pork insulin cannot be made to have the same DNA as human insulin – if it did it would no longer be pork insulin, so this statement is meaningless.

   'Human insulin is a replacement for pork insulin. Using the DNA that codes for human insulin, genetic engineering uses enzymes to insert this DNA into bacteria or yeast, which then produce the human protein.'

**3**  Use PEG, electric shock or particle gun method to insert DNA into rice protoplasts.

**4**  They are totipotent, so each transformed cell could grow into a new plant.

**5**  First isolate large amounts of the DNA coding for the salt-resistance proteins. You could either use cells that are producing large amounts of the protein and obtain the DNA from the mRNA via reverse transcriptase (see Figure 8.1); or make the DNA on a chemical synthesiser (if the sequence is fairly short).

   Wheat is a cereal and is not easily infected by *Agrobacterium*, so use the protoplast method. Treat wheat cells with cellulase and transform them by PEG fusion, electric shock treatment or the particle gun method (see Figure 8.2). Now grow the cells using tissue culture, adding plant hormones to stimulate root and shoot formation. Once plantlets have formed, they can be grown in an experimental greenhouse. You would then analyse the DNA from their tissue to see if they had taken up the gene for salt resistance. Finally, the plants would be grown under experimental conditions in soils of varying salinities.

Farmers having to cultivate low-lying marshy land or land reclaimed from the sea could benefit from the genetically engineered plants. Increased crop yields would improve their income and the food supply of local populations. The plants would be a stand-by for farmers who may be affected by flooding in the future.

The Pakistani farmers who had been cultivating the salt-resistant plants may demand a share in your profits. Your financial backers would want you to patent the plant to protect your rights. The general public would want to be reassured that it is safe to cultivate these plants in the environment and that they do not pose any unforeseen hazard.

6   To isolate proteins from milk, centrifuge to remove fat (it floats) and precipitate the proteins from the aqueous layer with ammonium sulphate, polyethylene glycol, or an organic solvent such as propanone. The crude protein is redissolved in buffer and then separated and purified by electrophoresis and/or chromatography. If you have an antibody to the human protein, just fix this onto a column of resin beads and pass the protein solution down the column. The required protein will bind tightly to its antibody and stay on the column, while all the others pass through. It can be removed from the column later with a solution that breaks the bonds between the protein and its antibody.

7   For blue roses, transfer the gene for blue flower colour from cornflowers to roses and at the same time turn off the genes that give roses their red (or pink or yellow) colour. Grow the transformed rose cells into plants by tissue culture.

For frost-resistant strawberries, look out for fruits that do well in cold climates. Isolate the genes responsible (probably several years' work). This has also been done by inoculating strawberry plants with genetically engineered bacteria that help the fruit to resist frost.

One of the main obstacles would be finding the genes that you would need to transfer to make your transgenic plants. Flower colour and cold resistance are probably controlled by more than one gene. It will be difficult to transfer several genes into plant cells.

If you are successful, you will face accusations of 'tampering with Nature'. People who feel strongly may pull up the plants on your experimental plots (this happened in the United States with trials on frost-resistant strawberries). You will also face legal barriers – you may have to wait a long time for permission to do field trials, for example. And you may find it hard to find someone to back your company financially if they are worried about the possible restrictions on your work. The general public may question whether blue roses are of any use, although they may be happy with the idea of home-grown strawberries all the year round – as long as the price is right.

## Chapter 9

1 (a) Lipase breaks down fat – intestinal lipases produce fatty acids from fats.
   (b) Polymerase forms a polymer from monomers, e.g. RNA polymerase.
   (c) Reductase catalyses donation of electrons or hydrogen atoms to a substrate – these enzymes are found in the electron transport chain of oxidative phosphorylation.
   (d) Ligase links two molecules together by condensation, e.g. DNA ligase.

2 Number the fibrinogen sequence from 1 to 20.
   (a) Trypsin cleaves between 12 and 13, between 15 and 16, and between 19 and 20.
   (b) Chymotrypsin cleaves between 8 and 9, and between 9 and 10.
   (c) Thrombin cleaves between 12 and 13.

3 If the residue mutates to a larger amino acid, this could block the entry of the substrate to the active site. If it mutates to a smaller one, the reverse could be true – the substrate might 'rattle around' in the active site and then diffuse away without reacting. Acidic or basic residues are often important in catalytic sites. If these residues change, e.g. if Asp (acidic) mutates to Asn (similar size, but neutral), all catalytic activity may be lost.

4 Haem contains iron, which is easily oxidised (to $Fe^{3+}$) or reduced (to $Fe^{2+}$) – this is a useful property for an enzyme involved in oxidation or reduction. NAD is a hydrogen carrier and aids dehydrogenases in removal of hydrogen atoms from substrates that are being oxidised.

5 Acidic amino acid residues – in fact, two aspartic acids are involved, one in the acid form (protonated), the other as aspartate (unprotonated).

6  Add more enzyme.

7  The support could bind the active site, or the binding could change the shape of the enzyme, distorting the active site.

8  Silk and wool are protein-based and could be degraded by proteases in the detergent. As enzymes are catalysts, they are not used up in a chemical reaction and are only needed in small amounts.

9  Papain breaks down myosin and collagen fibres in the meat, reducing stringiness and giving a softer texture.

## Bibliography

N. P. O. Green, G. W. Stout and D. J. Taylor, *Biological Science*, vols 1 and 2 (Cambridge, Cambridge University Press, 1990)

McCance and Widdowson, *The Composition of Foods*, 5th edn (London, Ministry of Agriculture, Fisheries and Food/Royal Society of Chemistry)

A. Manz *et al.*, Cancer mortality among workers in chemical plant contaminated with dioxin, *Lancet*, **303**, 19 October 1991

E. K. Watson *et al.*, Screening for carriers of cystic fibrosis through primary health care services, *Lancet*, **303**, 31 August 1991, pp. 504–7

D. J. Weatherall, *The New Genetics and Clinical Practice* (Oxford, Oxford University Press, 1991)

The *Newsletter of the National Centre for Biotechnology Education* (free with membership of the Schools' Biotechnology Club) is a useful source of tips and background material, as are the *School Science Review* and the *Journal of Biological Education*

# Index